CHARTING A HERO'S JOURNEY

Charting a Hero's Journey is a guide to the writing of a journal for college students engaged in volunteer community service and study abroad programs. It is based on the work of Joseph Campbell, who, in *The Hero with a Thousand Faces*, documented the universal myth of the hero's journey, and on the following writers, whose journals of study, living, travel, and service abroad are used extensively throughout the assignment:

> Jane Addams
> James Boswell
> Emily Bronson Conger
> Paul Cowan
> Sana Hasan
> Langston Hughes
> Samuel Johnson
> Mary Kingsley
> Kathleen Norris
> Octavio Paz
> Anthony C. Winkler

Linda A. Chisholm, BA, MA University of Tulsa; PhD Columbia University; DD (Hon) General Theological Seminary; LHD (Hon) Cuttington University College; University Fellowship, University of Surrey Roehampton; co-founder with Howard Berry of the Partnership for Service-Learning, Executive Vice President of the International Partnership for Service-Learning (1987–2002) and President of the International Partnership for Service-Learning and Leadership (2002–) ; founder and first General Secretary, Colleges and Universities of the Anglican Communion (1993–1997); and President of The Association of Episcopal Colleges (1985–2001).

Also by the author, with Howard A. Berry:

> *How to Serve and Learn Abroad Effectively:*
>   *Students Tell Students,* 1992
> *Service-Learning Around the World: An Initial Look,* 1998
> *Understanding the Education—And Through It the Culture—*
>   *in Education Abroad,* 2002

Kate Chisholm, BA, Yale University; MFA candidate, Towson University; theater director, writer and performer; recipient of the Richard Rodgers Award (American Academy of Arts and Letters) for the musical *The Hidden Sky,* written with her husband, composer/ lyricist Peter Foley.

CHARTING A HERO'S JOURNEY

by
Linda A. Chisholm

with illustrations by
Kate Chisholm

The International Partnership for Service-Learning and Leadership
New York

The International Partnership for Service-Learning and Leadership
815 Second Avenue, Suite 315
New York, New York 10017

LCCN 00-108177
ISBN 0-9701984-2-6

Book Design by Kate Chisholm

Printed on acid-free paper.

First Edition, Second Printing

To the memory of my parents and Kate's grandparents
Mary Kathryn Armstrong (1904–1963),
who taught me to love story, myth, and travel
and
Max George Armstrong (1894–1962),
dedicated public servant

and to the thousands of students of
The International Partnership for Service-Learning
who have traveled the hero's path

The hero ... is the man or woman who has been able to battle past his personal and local historical limitations.... Such a one's visions, ideas, and inspirations ... are eloquent, not of the present disintegrating society and psyche, but of the unquenched source through which society is reborn. His solemn task and deed ... is to return ... to us, transfigured, and teach the lesson he has learned of life renewed.

These deeply significant motifs of the perils, obstacles, and good fortunes of the way, we shall find ... in a hundred forms ... the everlastingly recurrent themes of the wonderful song of the soul's high adventure.

[E]ach who has dared to harken to and follow the secret call has known the perils of the dangerous, solitary transit.... [Yet] we have not ... to risk the adventure alone; for the heroes of all time have gone before us; the labyrinth is thoroughly known; we have only to follow the thread of the hero-path. And where we had thought to find an abomination, we shall find a god; where we had thought to slay another, we shall slay ourselves; where we had thought to travel outward, we shall come to the center of our own existence; where we had thought to be alone, we shall be with all the world.

Joseph Campbell, *The Hero with a Thousand Faces*

TABLE OF CONTENTS

Preface for Teachers and Advisers

Dear Teacher and Adviser,

Charting a Hero's Journey is designed as a guide for college and university students as they reflect upon their experience of travel, study, and living abroad and/or upon their work in community service. It may be used for the study of composition or, with adaptation, in first or final year seminars that examine the nature and process of college or university education. It is about a highly developed form of literature — the journal — and gives the student substantial practice in writing. It teaches the art of careful observation, accurate reporting and cross-cultural analysis. All of these are academic skills to be taught, learned, and credited.

But it is also something more.

- It provides an opportunity to bring coherence to the inner journey that occurs when students reflect upon a significant passage of their lives and the external journey they make into new situations.

- It is an aid for students as they search for meaning and direction in their lives.

- It is a means of making into a whole the fragments experienced in the current structures of higher education.

It is not an exposition on the process of learning, nor a sermon on the meaning of life. Rather, it is a call to the student to examine, direct, and document the transformation of self.

The book was designed specifically for participants in the semester, year, and summer programs of The International Partnership for

Service-Learning. These programs join substantive volunteer service and formal academic studies in such a way that the two parts complement and reinforce each other, adding up to more than the sum of the parts. In each of the eleven countries around the world in which the Partnership offers service-learning programs, students are asked to keep a journal of their experiences. *Charting a Hero's Journey* gives them a framework for their reflections and helps them see that, while their particular experiences and responses are unique, they are sharing a broad human experience with countless others past and present who have traveled a similar road.

It is based on the work of Joseph Campbell. In his now classic work *The Hero with a Thousand Faces*,[1] Campbell documented and explained the universal human tale, told in virtually every culture of the world and from time immemorial, of the young person who leaves the security of home to venture into the world. Along the road, the hero faces challenges, discovers the meaning of the journey, and returns home transformed.

In *Charting a Hero's Journey* I have extrapolated from the writings of Joseph Campbell twelve stages of the journey, describing each stage as it appears in the legends and myths of many cultures. Following the short description of each stage are excerpts from eleven superbly written journals by modern travelers, reflections of the authors upon the stage as experienced in their own journeys. Accompanying each excerpt are observations and questions for the student to ponder.

The journals I have chosen for inclusion were written by travelers to the locations of Partnership programs, but there are countless others that might have been quoted. As I read these and many other journals, I found that virtually every one contains passages that document each of the twelve stages of the journey, offering proof that Campbell was correct in naming the hero's journey a widely shared human experience. Teachers using the guide for the instruction of their students may use the passages here included or may wish to select passages from other journals.

For each stage, the student chooses one excerpt and the attached questions upon which to respond with a journal entry. By the end of the assignment the student has recorded in a series of thoughtful essays the whole of the journey, from the time of first deciding to embark on the hero's path to the return home.

But the construction of this guide to journal writing, like the mission and programs of The International Partnership for Service-Learning, has a broader purpose and applicability. *Charting a Hero's Journey* is a vehicle for integrating the learning that takes place through the new situations encountered along the road with the inner examination of meaning, values, and direction to which the journey gives rise. As the young hero-student analyzes what he is learning, he also documents the process of change within himself.

A historian by training and a college administrator by profession, I have long been fascinated by the writings of students about their own college experiences. While a graduate student at Columbia University in the 1970s, I read thousands of published and un-published letters and diaries written by American college students in the eighteenth, nineteenth, and twentieth centuries. Each generation has had its particular characteristics, responding in some way to the political and social circumstances of the time. And each student's experiences and reflections are unique according to his background, expectations, and bent. Nonetheless, there is a common progress that can be charted as students move from adolescence to adulthood.

We call the stage of our lives corresponding to the college years of traditional students the formative years, and for good reason. At this time childhood assumptions are questioned. The young person either appropriates the values and beliefs of his heritage or adopts new ones. Basic life patterns are established. The ways in which the young adult comes to think of herself are determining of her future. And so, in addition to introducing the student to Joseph Campbell and the hero story in history and legend, fostering skills of cross-cultural observation and analysis, and teaching the composition and literature of journal writing, *Charting a Hero's Journey* is designed to extend and deepen the student's notion of self.

It is my response to what seems to be a poverty of spirit in too many college students today. College and university professors around the world are deploring the loss of idealism in the current generation of students.[2] Defining themselves primarily as consumers who expect always to be thought "right" and to have others solve the problems they encounter, many students have failed through their narrow vision to see and live up to their potential as agents for good in our time. They have not taken up the challenges, either to themselves or to their societies. As educators, we have the responsibility and privilege to place before students a nobler vision of themselves, one that calls them to a higher purpose. This, it seems to me, is one important meaning of the *higher* learning to which we as college and university teachers have dedicated our lives.

While *Charting a Hero's Journey* may be used by students in traditional study abroad programs, in community service programs, and as a means of examining the very process of education, I want here to argue the case for service-learning. When I was first presented in the 1970s with the idea of joining academic study and volunteer community service into one pedagogy and one learning experience, I was immediately struck with the potential of service-learning to teach many valuable academic, social, and personal lessons simultaneously. The system of higher education that has evolved since the mid-nineteenth century in Europe, the Americas, and now throughout the world has many virtues. But its characteristics are fragmentation and compartmentalization. We have separated knowledge into disciplines and the university into departments. These structures discourage dialogue between adherents of the various disciplines and methodologies. Students are never asked to judge when a particular discipline and method is applicable and instructive, and when it is not. The result is that students — and perhaps even some of their teachers — mistake theoretical constructs for reality itself. They tend to see the discipline and method not as a way of ordering complex and often contradictory information, but as truth, whole and complete. The system of education we have designed closes minds to the possibility of other ways of knowing.

Equally limiting, our pedagogy and structures separate the learner from the learning, as if interpretations or even the choice of a line of inquiry can be divorced from the scholar's own historical moment and life history. Intellectual development occupies one sphere of the university, presided over by the faculty and academic dean; personal growth is relegated to another and separate sphere. The nineteenth-century college teacher was also counselor and guide for spiritual and personal issues and an example of moral as well as intellectual virtues. This pattern has long since been given up in favor of separation between the academic teacher and the professional specialist in student affairs. Of course, only intellectual development is recognized by the awarding of credit and finally by the degree, and thus is the only one understood to count. The two spheres are separate and certainly not equal.

The joining of academic study with volunteer service holds the promise to address the issues related to fragmentation and compartmentalization. By examining the ideas and issues encountered in a particular service experience from the viewpoint of various disciplines and methods, students are required to ask and answer the question of how a discipline does or does not shed light upon a real situation. The student must ask of art, sociology, economics, language, psychology, philosophy, biology, and other disciplines what each has to teach about a particular human condition or issue. Well-designed service-learning programs require that the student, in the mind's eye, walk around a real situation, looking at it from the vantage of various disciplines and methods, seeing it from different perspectives, judging the ability of each method to instruct, and finally bringing understanding into a whole.

Similarly, the union of academic study and service brings together personal life issues and decisions with intellectual development. The student involved in substantive service is moving out of the world of childhood in which he focused on his own personal concerns into the larger world, where he is called to take an active and productive role. Service redirects interest and energy from self-fulfillment alone to include the needs, issues, and perspectives of others. In doing so, the student finds purpose, meaning and vocation for himself, answering these life questions not in isolation but in the context of a community.

Furthermore, the student engaged in service is almost always working with those whose life circumstances are different from her own and who therefore approach issues differently. It may be, as in the case of Partnership students, in a new nation. But even those who serve in communities near campus or home encounter different social classes, ages, levels of education, and living conditions. The young and healthy student working with the infirm; the middle-class student serving among the rural or inner-city poor; the university student tutoring those who struggle for basic literacy — all challenge the student to see life from a different and broader perspective. The very heart of higher education, especially the liberal arts, lies in opening ourselves to see beyond our own individual experience. Our knowledge and understanding are extended by entering, however vicariously, the thoughts and experiences of others. The study of literature, history, religion, mathematics, and music allows us to share the mindset of those in other times and cultures. Combining formal study and immediate encounters with those who experience life differently brings a power to both. The service makes the academic study immediate and relevant as the study informs the service. Whether at home or abroad, the joining of study and service enlivens, enriches, and reinforces both, and helps the student use them in making life choices.

I close this introduction by reminding you that as teacher and adviser you have an important part in the story of the hero's journey. You may issue the call, act as mentor and guardian spirit along the way, and bestow the crown of laurels upon the hero's return. For good or ill, you may be the keeper of the gates. As you set your students on the hero's path, you seek to give them strong and trustworthy tools for the trip. I hope that *Charting a Hero's Journey* proves to be a useful compass for you and your students as they take up the challenges along the road, moving from the questions of what happened to the larger questions of what the journey means. The references to the great heroes of legend and history and the excerpts from the journals of other travelers invite the student as hero and you as mentor to join their company, accepting the tasks, persevering in the face of difficulties, discovering new wisdom and developing useful skills. The student-hero who is so transformed—Joseph Campbell would say transfigured—returns hoping for the affirmation of you who set him on his path, hoping that you see him now as an adult able to take up the leadership of the society. Yours is a noble calling, your soul's own high adventure. Do not see your work as anything less.

I wish to you, as well as to your students, Bon Voyage.

ACKNOWLEDGMENTS

I am indebted to Nancy Geyer Christopher, who first made me aware of the connection between the hero's journey as described by Joseph Campbell and the experience of students who leave home for service-learning. I had long puzzled about the difference between students returning from traditional study abroad programs, who, for the most part, report on what they saw, and those engaged in substantive service, who tend to focus on their own transformation. Nancy's son, Peter Geyer, had been a Partnership student, and in 1994 she presented a workshop on Campbell and the rite of passage to adulthood at the eleventh annual conference of The International Partnership, arguing the case that service could and should mark the passage from childhood to adulthood in our modern culture. Her book, *Right of Passage* (Washington: Cornell Press, 1996), deserves reading by anyone concerned with the issues of teaching and guiding young adults.

I also wish to thank the School of Theology, University of the South, Sewanee, Tennessee, for inviting me to campus as a Fellow-in-Residence, providing me with comforts and resources, including those of the excellent Jessie Ball DuPont Library, and thereby affording me the time and space to work on *Charting a Hero's Journey* without distraction.

Partial support for this project has been provided by the United States Department of State-supported Cooperative Grants Program of NAFSA: Association of International Educators.

I am grateful to the trustees and program directors of The Partnership from whom I have learned over the years and who supported this project; to Alex Tinari, Erika Ryser, Margaret Peckham Clark, and Kate Chisholm, who proved to be fine editors as well as computer experts and who obtained the permission to quote from the publishers and copyright holders of the excerpted journals; and to Kate Egan Norris for copyediting.

The content and design of the book was field-tested by International Partnership students. I am particularly indebted to Aaron Augustino of the University of Richmond, Katherine Smith of the University of New Hampshire, and Emily Winchell of Pacific Lutheran University for their insightful journals, critical analyses, and helpful suggestions.

Most especially, I value Howard Berry, founder and President of The International Partnership for Service-Learning, with whom I have been on a journey for eighteen years as we created and developed The International Partnership for Service-Learning, and who wrote the Afterword. He has both questioned and supported this project, adding his own keen insights and proving to be the best of mentors.

My guardian spirit is my husband, Alan Chisholm, who knows just when to make suggestions and when to leave me alone.

Finally, I thank the now almost four thousand Partnership students from over twenty nations who without the benefit of this guide followed the hero's path, striking out anew, accepting the challenges, slaying the beasts within themselves, humbly learning from their mistakes, discovering important boons, leaving a legacy of good work and good will, returning home to productive lives and leadership roles. We at The International Partnership for Service-Learning are proud of their accomplishments and appreciate their sharing their stories.

INTRODUCTION FOR STUDENTS

Dear Student,

This journal assignment, which you have already begun with your application essay and which you will continue during your semester or year of service-learning abroad, may turn out to be one of the most valuable educational experiences you have had. Previous Partnership students who have kept journals have told us this was true for them.

This assignment is about myths and legendary heroes, real-life journeys and journals. It is about a story told and retold in countless variations throughout human history and in virtually all cultures.

But it is not only *about* a story. It *is* a story—yours.

You will be telling your version of the universal tale, thereby expressing your individuality and enriching the story we all share.

In your journal you will be recording your observations of life in your host culture. You will be seeing and experiencing that life from many angles—your community service, your academic study, your living situation and your travel. We have arranged the program so that you meet people from many walks of life in order that you may know the richness, variety, contradictions and complexities of the country and culture you have chosen for your study and service abroad.

As you seek to understand your host culture, you will also be reflecting upon and probably wrestling with issues of your own life. In your journal you may be asking questions of purpose and meaning, beliefs and values, life choices and direction.

1

But while studying and serving in a new culture, you will not be just an observer standing on the sidelines as the academic tourist. Through your service and your interactions elsewhere, you will be a full participant, active and receptive. You will have an effect on others, and they and their culture will change you.

The external journey you make to a new land to face new challenges is both a metaphor for and the occasion of an interior journey. Not only *in* your host culture but *because of* it, you will uncover new dimensions in yourself. Through your service and study, the experiences you have, the relationships you build, and your focused reflection on it all, you will plumb new depths. You will discover your flexibility in adapting to new situations; your ability to analyze, investigate, compare and understand; your capacity to give to others and your willingness to receive; your independence and inter-dependence.

In most academic assignments you have had to date, you have been called on to be objective, to separate yourself from the subject and look on it as a disinterested observer. But in your journal you may — and indeed are urged to — express your own point of view. In the story told in your journal you are both narrator and protagonist, storyteller and hero. As hero, you will experience and reflect upon your own transformation. As storyteller, you record the process and your progression along the hero's path.

We hope that through your service-learning and study abroad you will find a new integration and coherence for yourself, bringing together what you are learning with who you are called to be and to become. Your journal will give voice to your experiences, ideas, feelings, and beliefs.

In the following pages you will learn about the universal story of the hero's journey and, through the journal excerpts, share in the journeys of others.

Here we would like to say a word about heroes, lest you resist applying the term to yourself. Heroes are not perfect and are generally not superhuman. Whether fictional or real, heroes are flawed. Think about stories you have read and characters that you identify as heroes. They blunder and stumble, sometimes making wrong choices, often lacking strength, intelligence, or will. At some stage along the way, they get in trouble and are saved only by the intervention of a friendly outside force. In short, heroes succeed and fail. You will too.

Your journal, then, should be honest. As you engage in this exercise—and it is an exercise in that it requires discipline, hard work, intelligence, faithfulness and concentration—the value for you will lie in admitting your mistakes and limitations and in accepting the mysteries for which there are no answers, or at least no answers now.

At the same time, claim your victories. When you have had an "Aha!" moment, when you have understood at last, when you know you have been of service, when you have been a gracious guest, when you have conquered a fear or anxiety, when you have exercised more patience than you thought humanly possible, when you have shown good judgment, imagination, intelligence, and persistence, record your triumphs.

Tell your story.

Bon Voyage!

THE MONOMYTH OF THE HERO'S JOURNEY

A Story

Once upon a time, in a far-off kingdom, the citizens were worried. Their ruler, who was both wise and foolish, benevolent and tyrannical, just and unjust, was aging. Who would assume the leadership of the kingdom when the ruler passed from the stage? Who would be the guardian of laws and ideals, the bearer of fresh energy, the source of new ideas?

Now most went about their daily rounds tending home and farm, factory and office, remembering only occasionally their concern about the future, believing it would take care of itself.

But there was One, restless with things as they were, longing to construct the world anew. So One set out to discover the world, leaving behind the familiar and secure.

At times along the way, One walked elysian fields, drinking from pure springs, resting in gentle meadows, and led by sure-footed guides.

But at other times, the way was hard. There were gates guarded by fierce creatures through which One had to pass. And beyond there were mountains to climb, dragons to slay, and trails to blaze.

One was faced with new and difficult tasks, testing One's courage, endurance, strength, imagination, intelligence, commitment, good humor, and good will.

Thus One journeyed, returning finally to the kingdom where the road began.

But One was not the same, nor was the kingdom. One had been transfigured by the journey and the old ruler had not gotten any younger. It was clear that succession was near.

Some citizens of the kingdom proposed that One should lead them to the future. "One has been to parts unknown. One has done battle with the beasts and returned victorious." "No," said others, "One is imperfect still. There are beasts not yet slain. The boon One brings back is untested. One is not fully formed and transformed."

"But," spoke up Future, "One has brought back new visions, new wisdom, new skills. Citizens, you cannot be certain that under One's leadership you will live happily ever after, but, after all, One is the best you have. You must entrust me to One's hands."

And so it was.

THE STORY

You have never heard or read that particular tale before, but you have heard and read countless versions of it.

The earliest fairy tales told to you as a child; your college classes in history, literature, religion, anthropology, and the arts; and many favorite and famous movies recount the adventures of the young person who leaves behind the familiar to strike out into new territory. Finding there some special secret or good, he eventually returns home, bringing the discovered boon to others.

The variations are endless. In some stories the hero is a man, in others a woman. The journey may begin with a clear inner call or merely by accident or chance. A few stories end prematurely when the would-be hero rejects the opportunity before him.

For those who accept the challenge, the journey may be by land or by sea. En route, there are difficulties and challenges — rivers to ford, deserts to cross. There are angels to wrestle with and dragons to slay. There are feats to perform and puzzles to solve.

Sometimes the course is clearly charted. At other times the hero must make her own map as she enters new territory. In most versions there are guardian spirits in one form or another who guide the way and protect her from danger, often snatching the hero from the jaws of defeat just in the nick of time.

The climax comes when the hero arrives at the place she has been seeking, the magical moment when the purpose of the journey is revealed. Enlightenment comes, the boon is uncovered, the good which the hero set out or was destined to find is now in her possession.

A few heroes remain wanderers forever. But most return, bringing back their discoveries and the stories of their adventures to share with those remaining at home.

In most stories the returning hero is crowned with laurels, wins the prize, and is acknowledged as leader.

JOSEPH CAMPBELL

It was the scholar and teacher Joseph Campbell (1904–1987) who, after reading myths and stories told in cultures all over the world and from ages long past to the present, realized and wrote about the universality of this tale of the hero's journey. Appropriating a word which James Joyce had used in *Finnegan's Wake*, Campbell called the tale of the hero's journey the "monomyth," each version being but an elaboration of the single, simple formula of separation-initiation-return.[3]

In his now classic work *The Hero with a Thousand Faces*, Campbell not only recounted from the world's religions and mythologies the journeys of dozens of heroes, but sought to unearth the meaning of the symbolism contained in these stories. The tales are more than exciting adventures. They tell, through metaphor, the story of the journey we all must make from dependent childhood to autonomous adulthood. In this all-important journey of life, we discover our purpose and define our individual identity.

As in the allegorical journeys of myth and legend, we face a series of challenges and tests, and at each stage we make decisions, consciously or unconsciously, to go forward or turn back. Throughout the journey there are opportunities to confront our previously-held assumptions, to conquer our doubts and anxieties, to accept responsibility, and to press on to a new and broader understanding of human life, both our own life and the lives of others.

For those who persevere, there are discoveries that make life richer and more fulfilling. And like the great heroes, we find a boon that we bring back for the good of our families, communities, nations, and world. As we examine beliefs and values, ideas and visions, we struggle with the questions of how we will choose to live our lives, where our energies will be directed, what qualities will characterize our relationships with others, and for what purpose we are living.

Joseph Campbell helps us, then, to understand the appeal of these stories of heroes' journeys and their lasting place in our respective cultures. For, explains Campbell, these are not merely tales of past glories but tales which serve to illuminate our present corporate and personal realities.

The external journey to a new land, meeting new people, encountering new ways of thinking and organizing human life is paralleled by the internal journey to redefine, extend, and deepen our notion of ourselves. The external journeys of others may become the means for examining our own internal change and progress.

But the external journeys of heroes recounted in the timeless tales are more than symbolic means of expressing inward transformation. They are also the causes of it, for the hero and for future generations. The word "metaphor" means bearer of or translator of truth. The journeys of two great heroes help us to understand the concept.

Moses, discontent with life in Egypt, envisioned a better world. Leading his people from slavery, he endured with them danger and hardship, crossing the Red Sea with the Egyptian army on their heels, and then wandering in the desert in search of the promised land. "Would we not have been better remaining in the flesh pots of Egypt?" the people asked Moses. But he persevered and they with him, until they came at last to Mount Sinai. Having ascended the mountain alone, Moses returned to deliver to his people a new set of laws by which they should live, laws which ever since have inspired people to seek a social order based not on the rule of power but on equity and self-control.

The implication is clear. Had Moses chosen to remain in Egypt, had he not crossed the great divide of the Red Sea, had he been unwilling to experience the trials and uncertainties of the desert, he would not have been able and ready to receive the greater and loftier vision of human life as expressed in the Ten Commandments. His life was transformed by his journey. The lives of countless generations after him have been inspired by his journey, his reflection, and his gift.

Siddhartha also journeyed forth, despite his rich father's best efforts to circumscribe the young prince's world. Some would have said Siddhartha had everything anyone might want in the vast and lavish kingdom he would one day inherit. Why should he ever leave its comforts and privileges?

But Siddhartha was curious and reflective. Choosing the hero's path, he encountered along the road people and conditions he previously had not known existed. Witnessing death, illness, and old age for the first time, he wrestled with what these had to teach him about life and its meaning. Finally, through the teaching of a monk, he understood that he must seek the truth, and so followed the trail and eventually become the Buddha—the Enlightened One. Like Moses, he was transformed by what he encountered on his journey away from home, and so have those who have since sought and followed his path.

We may imagine these two stories and those of other heroes ending differently. Had Siddhartha and Moses not ventured forth to meet the new, or persisted in the midst of confusion and discouragement, they would not have arrived at new understanding.

But it was not the journey alone that led them to wisdom. It was their readiness to learn from their experiences and their ability to ponder that prepared the way for them to receive, discover, and formulate new truths.

And so the outward action and experiences of the journey and the inward reflection together form the transforming experience. They are an organic whole.

The most dramatic journey we make in life is that of young adulthood. These years of our lives are called the formative years for good reason. It is at this time that we move from an identity largely determined by parents, extended family, inherited religion, political values, and cultural mores to become our unique selves. It is in these years that we either accept inherited values for ourselves or formulate new ones. Making decisions about careers and partners, we set basic patterns by which we live out our lives.

In many cultures, the hero's journey is ritualized as a rite of passage marking the shift from childhood to adulthood. In these rites the young person is physically removed from family and community and put through study and training that culminates in a series of tests. When he succeeds in passing these tests, he is returned to the village, but now having a new place. No longer thought of as or treated like a child, the young person takes his place in the adult community.

And, by way of introduction to the idea of the hero's journey, one final word. We continue throughout life to read and be inspired by stories of heroes and their journeys because, while young adulthood may be the most dramatic and concentrated of journeys, it is not the only one we make in life. As we learn new things, meet new people, take different jobs, move to new communities, establish new relationships, assume new responsibilities, leave behind the familiar past, and go from one stage of life into another, we use these events to reflect and change, and grow. There are always new challenges, new boons to be discovered, and recurring opportunities to return the boon for the good of others.

As you are challenged by the journeys of other heroes, so others will benefit from reading your version. Because the reflections of fellow travelers are stimuli for examining the meaning of our own journey, your elders as well as your successors will learn from yours.

JOURNALS AND JOURNAL WRITING

Journals are a special and an especially satisfying form of literature because they recount a person's experience and interpretation close to the time of the experience. Unlike novels, stories, essays, poetry, research papers, or memoirs which record conclusions after prolonged reflection, a journal commands the writer and invites the reader into the very process through which new thinking is derived and change occurs.

The very human desire to preserve for one's self and for others the experiences of one's own life has motivated diarists in virtually all cultures and in widely varying circumstances. Especially eager are those aware that they are in the midst of transforming events. War and grief have inspired the keepers of journals; but equally and more happily, so have journeys, whether for work or pleasure, study or service, adventure or recovery from illness or sadness. Soon-to-be travelers realize that new sights and new insights will make them into different people. Many who decide to chart their journey begin the journal before leaving home in order to capture the change they feel is bound to take place in them.[4]

Most diarists welcome the opportunity to share the progress of their journey with others. Writing a journal "is often a kind of confession, and no confession is effective unless another hears it!"[5] Hence, the journal as a literary form has been cultivated and highly developed in the hands of skilled writers. But skilled as a writer or not, the journalist elicits our empathy by inviting us along as companions on the journey. If that journey is also in the nature of the hero's journey, then the sharing between narrator and reader is all the more intimate, since the hero's journey is a life story in which we all participate.

Your Journal

The assignment is constructed as it is in order to:

- teach you about myth and metaphor in culture and literature, and ways you may use them to enrich your own life and your writing;
- introduce you to the ideas of Joseph Campbell, one of the most prominent, if controversial, scholars of our time;
- expose you to the lives of eleven people whose writing and actions influenced their times, some of whom influence our own;
- demonstrate to you that, broadly speaking, your experience is part of a universal human experience;
- illustrate the variety of responses possible at each stage of the journey;
- allow you to examine and preserve in writing the uniqueness of your life and reflections;
- set before you examples of good writing and, through practice, develop your own writing ability;
- hone your skills in observing carefully, probing deeply, and recording accurately;
- give you a way of seeing your education and growth progressively and coherently.

The journal in which you will record your experiences and reflections along the path follows, more or less, the stages of the classic tale of the hero's journey. The twelve stages have been extrapolated from the writings of Joseph Campbell, but do not follow strictly his schema. While every story has a beginning, middle, and end, there is within the general framework considerable latitude. You should become familiar with the stages, then focus on and write about the one relevant at a given time in your experience of studying and serving abroad.

Each of the twelve stages begins with a brief description of the stage and illustrates a few of the endless variations. The richness of the tale and the key to its universality lie in its variations. While putting your experience in the context of the universal experience of the hero's journey, you are urged to identify and record the particulars of your own journey.

The Excerpted Journals of Others

Accompanying the description of each stage are excerpts from real-life journals written about journeys. Collectively they cover the period from 1775 to the present and represent a wide variety of authors, destinations and purposes of their journeys, and writing styles. The quoted passages include those that focus on issues of the external journey, those in which the author is primarily concerned with the internal journey, and those that skillfully weave both together. Some are lyrical and highly reflective; others descriptive and objective. They include the philosophical, expansive, theoretical, satirical, sober, humorous, angry, and contented. Some reflect high and clear purpose; others express confusion and lack of direction. All are set in a particular place and in a particular period in history, reflecting both the terrain of the journey and the interests and issues of the times. All are well-written; some are considered literary masterpieces.

Some relate to the experience of research and study abroad, others to service, a few to a returning to the writer's root culture, and all to the experience of living in a new or changed culture. Two of the writers became so tied to the new land that they stayed, making it home; others considered the land to which they traveled their second nation, returning as often as possible. Others found the experience useful but had no desire to return again. At least two returned home discouraged and disillusioned. All were surprised by what they found in the new land and in themselves. None remained unchanged by the journey; some reveal a deep transformation.

Of the thousands of journals possible for selection, the ones chosen for this volume were written by people who traveled to or from a country in which there are or have been programs of The International Partnership for Service-Learning. As you become familiar with these journals and as you construct your own, remember that around the globe are service-learning students writing journals, having experiences and reactions similar to and different from yours, and that each is traveling the hero's path as are you.

INSTRUCTIONS FOR THE ASSIGNMENT

Following each excerpt are questions stimulated by the passage itself. These questions are not meant to define your journey but rather to be a springboard for your thinking and reflection. Within each stage there are eight to eleven quoted passages, and you may select the one(s) to which you will re-spond with your own journal entry. Some passages and writers will appeal to you more than others.

In the Annotated Bibliography in the back of the book, you will find a one-page précis of the author's life to help you place the quoted material in context. You should refer to these often and become familiar with these eleven authors. Although they lived and traversed the hero's path in different times and places, they are fellow-travelers on the road. You will find them good, if at times provocative, companions.

Before you begin writing, read the introductory material on the hero's journey, the writing of journals, and this section of instructions for completing the assignment. Study the description of each stage on the first pages of each chapter so that you have a sense of the stages and the progress of the journey before you begin writing. Start to make yourself familiar with the excerpted journals by reading the one-page summaries of each in the Annotated Bibliography.

If you are not already familiar with the work of Joseph Campbell, you may wish to read *The Hero with a Thousand Faces*, but it is not required for the assignment.

You would do well to think about and keep a running list of stories you know from legend or history that follow the pattern of the hero's journey. Countless fairy tales and children's literature such as *Alice in Wonderland, The Chronicles of Narnia, A Wrinkle in Time, The Wind in the Willows,* and even *Winnie the Pooh* are hero stories. The great legends of Greek and Roman mythology, including *The Odyssey* of Homer; many stories in the Bible; the Arthurian legend; *Beowulf; Chanson de Roland; El Cid; the Nibelungenlied; Don Quixote;* and Dante's *Divine Comedy* are but a few classics of the Western World that follow the model of the hero's journey.

Similar legends are to be found in cultures all around the world. The Gilgamesh legend from the Tigris -Euphrates Valley, *The Seven Voyages of Sinbad the Sailor* from Persia, *The Journey to the West* from China, Rama's search for Sita from India, and the White Buffalo Calf Woman legend of the Lakota/Dakota indigenous peoples of North America are only a few of the thousands of classic tales of quest that have shaped civilizations.

And, lest this seem an exercise of the past, think of today's movies that follow the basic pattern of the hero's journey. *Star Wars* springs readily to mind, but as with legend, history, and literature, there are more examples than one can count.

As you recall these stories, try to think metaphorically. Ask yourself what the images presented by the storyteller, novelist, historian, or filmmaker are meant to represent and convey.

CONSTRUCTING YOUR JOURNAL

You are required to submit a total of twenty entries, including at least one for each stage of the journey. You may choose any of the excerpts within a stage for your response. Since there are twelve stages, you will then select another eight excerpts and related questions about which to write. These eight may all be related to one stage or chosen from a number of stages. Each entry should be from one substantial paragraph to three pages in length.

Each should be a response to one of the excerpted passages. The questions following the passages are not meant to prescribe, but rather to stimulate your thinking. You will probably not want to answer all of the questions under a single entry. Choose the questions that interest you the most. Your response should be thoughtful, and as revealing and reflective as you can make it.

Please help your reader by indicating for each of your entries to which stage and excerpt you are referring. Write the name of the stage and the author's last name on the upper right corner of the page.

Assemble the journal for reading by your teacher in the order of the stages as they appear in the Table of Contents.

You will be graded on your thoughtfulness, your observation, the clarity of your writing, and on the knowledge of your host culture that you will have gained from your academic studies and from your experiences.

TIPS ON WRITING YOUR JOURNAL

While there is a suggested sequence for entries and there are identifiable stages of the journey, your own experience and choice may make it desirable to follow a somewhat different sequence. Make yourself familiar with the general description of the stages. Then, when you have an important experience or insight, feel free to turn to that stage and write your entry. You are encouraged to circle back as your experience grows, adding perspectives that you did not possess at an earlier period. A good way to do this is to let the original entry stand as first written, and then add paragraphs, noting which of your reflections came later in the program.

You are encouraged, but not required, to respond to the excerpts of different authors. Each is unique in outlook and writing style. As you reread the journal summaries, and as you move through the assignment reading the excerpted passages, you will become familiar with each author's story and writing.

The quoted passages reflect the two sides of the journey — the interior journey and the exterior one. Your own entries may concentrate on one or the other, though in the richest journals the two are mingled.

TIMING THE WRITING OF YOUR ENTRIES

One purpose of the assignment is for you to track the progress of the change that is occurring in you. In order to do this, you must begin your writing early in the program and keep on writing until the end. You will not produce a good journal if you wait until the last days and try to do it all at once, any more than writing a term paper in one sitting produces a satisfactory paper.

You should write entries for the first four stages (Hearing the Call, Preparing for the Journey, Departing and Separating, and Crossing the First Threshold) in the first two to three weeks. Write entries for stages V through IX (Taking up the Challenges, Battling the Beasts, Passing through the Gates, Recognizing Guides and Guardian Spirits, and Celebrating the Victories) during the middle weeks of the program. The final entries (Discovering the Boon, Charting the Course, Returning Home) should be the focus of your reflection and writing in the last weeks of the program.

Once at home, we hope you will want to add additional entries to the experience of Returning Home. You may wish to do this several weeks, several months and several years after your return. Unlike the impression formal schooling sometimes conveys, learning from an important experience never needs to cease. The more experiences we have and the more we ponder the meaning of our experience, the richer and deeper our reflection becomes and the more useful in guiding our beliefs, decisions, and actions.

You will, of course, continue your journey as long as you live. Each added experience will enhance your understanding of your past, just as present experience prepares the road to an enriched future.

FURTHER CLUES TO (ANY) JOURNAL WRITING

Literary journal writing is not the same as keeping a personal diary of daily thoughts and activities. Nor is a good journal a series of unconnected thoughts. Rather, it reflects upon what anthropologists call "critical incidents" — those moments in which a particular issue or cultural puzzle is encapsulated — and upon what they have to teach. You will know critical incidents when you experience them, for they wake you up, sometimes rudely. Critical incidents are the times of challenge or victory when your notion of what is or should be is turned upside down, or when puzzle pieces fall into place. Your thinking and action take on a new perspective. These moments are the signposts and often the milestones along the hero's road.

Because your journal is a literary one, to be read by others, you will realize that among the skills you must bring are keen powers of observation, a willingness to look into yourself to understand how you and your new world intersect, and the power to communicate through the written word.

Many writers and journalists believe there is no better aid than a little notebook carried with you at all times. Abraham Lincoln called his notebook his "ammunition box," his place for jotting down events, ideas, conversations, and feelings as they occurred. If you do the same, you will find these rough notes become the raw material from which you will later construct a journal entry. Writer Joan Didion refers to her book of notes as her "bankbook for the mind," a forgotten account accumulating interest which then "pays her passage to the world back there."[6] If you like to draw, add sketches to remind you of a particular happening. Allow your notebook to be cluttered—and accept the fact that much of the material will remain unused. Planted in your notebook, these seeds of memory will germinate for a fruitful journal entry, or die a natural death.

As you meet another culture, one of your primary challenges is that of separating assumptions based on your own background from those on which the host culture is based. The notebook and the journal are excellent places to hone your skills.

As you keep your notebook, practice the art of accurate observation. Try describing a person or scene in as much detail as possible, then go back and underline every word which reflects *your* judgment and values. Think through these words that you have so freely used. Ask yourself how your judgments have been culturally conditioned, and who might agree or disagree with your opinion and why. In your mind's eye, walk around the situation to catch a glimpse from another perspective. Learning to enter the mindset of another extends the limits of our own experience and, finally, is what is liberating about a liberal arts education. "A person of broad sympathies" is a phrase used to describe an educated person. Learning to empathize with others and to look upon them with compassion is an ultimate purpose of higher learning, study abroad and community service.

When the time comes to write the journal entry, review your notes and read through the excerpts in the stage about which you plan to write. You may need to refresh your memory by reviewing the summaries of the quoted journals in the Annotated Bibliography.

Select the excerpt and the related questions to which you will respond. Reflect on the passage, and plan the content of your response. Study the style of the excerpt and decide the style and format of your response. Pay attention to the writing styles of the quoted authors, and when you have decided how you will respond, choose a writing style that complements your content. As in all literary works, your entries should be composed, as opposed to your just writing as thoughts come to you. Remember that even James Joyce labored over his stream of consciousness! Describing an actual occurrence and then interpreting it is better than giving only general impressions.

Among the many possibilities for the style of journal entries are:

- a factual description of any event and its various meanings to those involved;
- a comparison between a current event and past event;
- reflection upon a personal experience or on an idea, cultural practice, or situation;
- a conversation reflecting the ideas and personalities of two or more persons, or between two sides of yourself;
- a letter, poem, or parable.

Be aware of the analogies and metaphors in the excerpt. In your own writing use such images, but do so deliberately and consistently within a single entry.

Remember that the most difficult entries to write, but often the most successful, are short. See how much you can say in as few words as possible.

Be honest, be specific, and be clear.

But above all, enjoy this rarity in the academic enterprise — writing about yourself.

STAGE I

HEARING
THE CALL

Each hero's journey begins with a call to leave behind the familiar and to venture into parts unknown. The call may come suddenly, as it did in the form of a blinding light to Saul (later known as Saint Paul) on the road to Damascus, or it may unfold gradually. It may be intentional and deliberate, the result of a chance meeting, or even a blunder. Sometimes it is enforced, as generations of young men learned when they received a notice calling them to active duty in the army. The call may be clearly recognized or but dimly perceived. Often the call is best recognized only in retrospect.

The herald of the call may be an idea or series of ideas, an event or series of events, or an encounter or a series of encounters with a person, persons, or a group. The crisis of the herald's appearance is, says Joseph Campbell, "the call to adventure,"[7] as it was for King Arthur, who began the search for the Holy Grail by chasing a hart.

The hero thus called may react in varying ways—by accepting immediately, by delaying temporarily, by retreating, or by refusing altogether. But unless the response is outright refusal, as it was for Daphne in the Greek legend, "the call rings up the curtain, always, on a mystery of transfiguration—a rite, or moment of spiritual passage which, when completed, amounts to a dying and a birth."[8]

JANE ADDAMS

I recall an incident which must have occurred before I was seven years old, for the mill in which my father transacted his business that day was closed in 1867. The mill stood in the neighboring town adjacent to its poorest quarter. Before then I had always seen the little city of ten thousand people with the admiring eyes of a country child, and it had never occurred to me that all its streets were not as bewilderingly attractive as the one which contained the glittering toyshop and the confectioner. On that day I had my first sight of the poverty which implies squalor, and felt the curious distinction between the ruddy poverty of the country and that which even a small city presents in its shabbiest streets. I remember launching at my father the pertinent inquiry why people lived in such horrid little houses so close together, and that after receiving his explanation I declared with much firmness when I grew up I should, of course, have a large house, but it would not be built among the other large houses, but right in the midst of horrid little houses like these.

That curious sense of responsibility for carrying on the world's affairs which little children often exhibit because "the old man clogs our earliest years," I remember in myself in a very absurd manifestation. I dreamed night after night that every one in the world was dead excepting myself, and that upon me rested the responsibility of making a wagon wheel. The village street remained as usual, the village blacksmith shop was "all there," even a glowing fire upon the forge and the anvil in its customary place near the door, but no human being was within sight. They had all gone around the edge of the hill to the village cemetery, and I alone remained alive in the deserted world. I always stood in the same spot in the blacksmith shop, darkly pondering as to how to begin, and never once did I know how, although I fully realized that the affairs of the world could not be resumed until at least one wheel should be made and something started. Every victim of nightmare is, I imagine, overwhelmed by an excessive sense of responsibility and the consciousness of a fearful handicap in the effort to perform what is required; but perhaps never were the odds more heavily against "a warder of the world" than in these reiterated dreams of mine.

Twenty Years at Hull-House, 8–10

For some heroes the call comes very early in life. Many people have memories of early experiences, ambitions or, like Addams, suggestive dreams, that they later understand to have been strivings toward meaning, purpose and vocation. There are career counselors who believe that every person's search for a career should begin by recalling and examining her earliest ideas and games of pretend about what she wanted to be when she grew up.

 Have you any such memories? Can you trace a path, however winding, from your early longings to your decision to participate in the service-learning program?

 Do you remember your first encounter with poverty or other human need or pain? Did you feel any responsibility toward the people who were suffering or did they seem to come from an alien world, far removed from your own? Did you talk with anyone about your observations, feelings, questions? Do you remember the response?

LANGSTON HUGHES

It was ten o'clock, on a June night, on the S.S. *Malone,* and we were going to Africa. At ten o'clock that morning I had never heard of the S.S. *Malone,* or George, or Ramon, or anybody else in its crew of forty-two men. Nor any of the six passengers. But now, here were the three of us laughing very loudly, going to Africa.

I had got my job at a New York shipping office. Ramon got his job at another shipping office. But George just simply walked on board about supper time. A Filipino pantry boy got mad and quit at the last moment. Naturally, the steward didn't want to sail short-handed. He saw George hanging around the entrance to the pier, watching the stevedores finish loading. The Filipino steward said: "Hey, colored boy! You, there! You want a job?" And George said: "Yes," so he walked on board, with nothing but a shirt and a pair of overalls to his back, and sailed.

Now, he lay there in his bunk, laughing about his landlady. He said she intended to put him out if he didn't find a job. And now that he had found a job, he wouldn't be able to tell her for six months. He wondered if she knew Africa was six months away from Harlem.

"*Largo viaie,*" said Ramon.

The Big Sea, 5

For some people the call is many years in forming, and when the move to begin the hero's journey is made it is from clear motivation, high purpose, and ideals. But not always. While few would embark as causally as Langston Hughes, Ramon, and George did, many answer a call on short notice and without great clarity about inner or even outward destination.

 Where on the continuum do you fit? Was your call more like that of Langston Hughes or that of previously quoted Jane Addams?

 Hughes's friend George left his rent unpaid. What are you leaving unfinished?

MARY KINGSLEY

It was in 1893 that, for the first time in my life, I found myself in possession of five or six months which were not heavily forestalled, and feeling like a boy with a new halfcrown, I lay about in my mind, as Mr. Bunyan would say, as to what to do with them. "Go and learn your tropics," said Science. Where on earth am I to go, I wondered, for tropics are tropics wherever found, so I got down an atlas and saw that either South America or West Africa must be my destination, for the Malayan region was too far off and too expensive. Then I got Wallace's *Geographical Distribution* and after reading that master's article on the Ethiopian region I hardened my heart and closed with West Africa. I did this more readily because while I knew nothing of the practical condition of it, I knew a good deal both by tradition and report of South East America, and remembered that Yellow Jack was endemic, and that a certain naturalist, my superior physically and mentally, had come very near getting starved to death in the depressing society of an expedition slowly perishing of want and miscellaneous fevers up the Parana.

Travels in West Africa, 1

Mary Kingsley had spent the years of her twenties caring for parents. Upon their death, she found herself with time on her hands. Her choice of Africa, an outrageous choice in her time for a single woman, was based on interests but also on the impossibility of other locations.

 How did you choose the location for your study abroad and your service-learning? Who or what influenced your choice? To what extent were you motivated by having a time in your life with nothing to do?

 Why did you choose to leave the physical, intellectual, and emotional comforts of home to face new challenges? Did you, like Mary Kingsley, feel "like a boy with a new halfcrown?" If not, how did you feel?

ANTHONY WINKLER

I had always wanted to go home. I did not wish to spend the rest of my days in the company of Americans, for as a whole I did not understand them and was certain that I never would. There were a few whom I thought I understood, but it was with the shallow grasp of book-learning rather than the deeper understanding that springs from the heart.

Living in America as an immigrant was for me like living in a vivid dream. Sometimes things were briefly clear, you saw this and that and why so-and-so was so, but then abruptly the picture would change and you would feel giddy at your own denseness. It was like walking into a movie that was half over and picking up the storyline in the middle. Some things you got from the context, others escaped you. The despair of it all was that you could never see the movie from the start and so were forever doomed only to dimly understand it.

I felt no love for the land. It did not smell right. Even after thirteen years it still had the alien, unrecognizable spoor of a foreign place. It did not smell of labouring bodies, burning cane fields, and animal dung, and smell that way whether in the windless heat of noon or in the feathery cool breezes of the evening the way Jamaica did. Instead, it had the odour of things man-made and lifeless—store bought clothes or the felt of a new hat. "Every fox likes the smell of his own hole," Grandfather used to say. I did not like the smell of America.

It did not sound right. During the daylight hours the Jamaica of my childhood had rattled like a dray cart loaded with pots and pans, giving off the constant clatter of disorder and poverty. Nights rang with the sounds of the unseen creatures that roosted in the bushes and trees—the whistling frogs, crickets, croaking lizards—mixed in with the barking of dogs, the cough of a passing car, the throb of a distant sound system pounding like a feral heart.

But the America in which I lived hummed with the orderly rhythm of an electric clock. At night it shrieked sporadically of fire, accident, heart attack, robbery and murder. Everywhere around Los Angeles, no matter where you laid your head at night, you heard a sleepless rumble from the arterial highways that lanced through the city. Sometimes at night I would awaken and hear that droning sound and my mind would turn to the thousands of cars and trucks hurtling down the highways, and I would wonder where they were going, what people rode in them, what stories they had to tell, and that would be the end of sleep for me....

Still, I would go home. And I would go home, perhaps not in glory and triumph, but with laurels enough to show that I had waged a good fight in America.

I was finally a published writer. I was the author of three college textbooks, two of which were selling so well that my first royalty cheque had been the equivalent of a year's salary. If my wishes had come true, I would have returned home with my novels dripping from my coat pockets, my plays appearing to rave reviews on Broadway, my poetry being recited in English classes, but it was clear that none of this was going to happen. All I had to show for my twelve years in America were three college textbooks and a year's salary in the bank. Yet it was enough. Not glory, perhaps, but workmanlike accomplishment that Louise or any of the other stalwart women of my childhood would have applauded. Older and wiser, I would settle for less, call a truce with my ambition, and go home.

I decided that I would go home to teach. There was such a desperate shortage of teachers in Jamaica that the government had lately launched an overseas recruitment programme. The recruiters had canvassed Los Angeles the year before but had fared badly because the pay was dreadful and the chief allurement—life in a sunny tourist haven for a year or two— did not have much appeal to Angelenos who had their own benign climate. Jamaica was also getting bad press at the time because of Manley and his well-publicized admiration of Castro. The island, it was said, could end up in the communist orbit. Moreover, there were rumours of an anti-white groundswell on the island that had resulted in some ugly behaviour towards tourists.

Nevertheless, my plan struck me as sensible, and I was especially proud that by teaching I could possibly do some tangible good. I would return home to give back, not to take.

Going Home to Teach, 3–4, 16–17

Anthony Winkler honestly acknowledges two motivations for his return to teach in his native Jamaica. The first was his desire to get away from the America to which he remained alien despite an American mother and grandmother, thirteen years, and notable success in his field of teaching and writing. The second motive prompting his decision was a genuine desire to help Jamaica. Most of us have complex motives.

 Was the desire to get *away* part of your call? If so, from what or from whom?

 To what were you drawn?

PAUL COWAN

In 1961, after John Kennedy's Inauguration, progressive ideas became a little more popular in Cambridge. I had a special, private reason for believing that Kennedy was more sensitive to problems like segregation than the Harvard professors he had named as his advisers. He was a member of a minority group and he had graduated from Choate. My fantasy was that his apparent concern for the poor had grown out of the same bitter dislike of the Protestant elite that I had developed during my years at boarding school. When he urged people to "ask not what your country can do for you—ask what you can do for your country," I wanted to believe that he was talking about an America that included poor people, sensitive young people, liberal adults, but excluded the selfish bigots he and I had both known at Choate.

Soon his Presidency would inspire thousands of young people like me to leave their middle-class environments and work in the Peace Corps or the civil-rights movement. But not quite yet. At Harvard that year hundreds of students, suddenly awakened to political awareness, joined a campus organization called Tocsin that was working for nuclear disarmament. It took us into libraries and lecture halls, not to the ghettos and barrios where some of us would be forced to redefine our political identities a few years hence. We sought to master all the relevant scientific information so that we could devise practical suggestions for arms reduction and pass them along to men like McGeorge Bundy. The most gentlemanly form of protest imaginable, it was based on the assumption that a rational dialogue between Harvard faculty and Harvard students would save the world from destruction. Still, many undergraduates considered Tocsin extremely radical that year, especially when we staged public demonstrations. So we spent a great deal of time arguing with the conservatives on campus about issues like underground testing and phased inspections systems.

But those technical subjects seemed dull and irrelevant to me, though I was ashamed to admit it. It was the same conflict I had felt on the *Crimson* and in my courses, a conflict that seemed to be afflicting dozens of my friends, too. The fact that our educations seemed pointless, unrelated to any future we could imagine, made us feel especially guilty, for it meant that we were unable to make use of the magnificent opportunities that Harvard was supposed to offer all of its undergraduates. The guilt produced an alarming kind of paralysis. Ever since my freshman year many of the people I knew rarely went to class, never studied, spent a great deal of time worrying about the nervous breakdown that always seemed to be one frustration away. As a result our conversations were often elliptical forms of self-mockery. We discussed ourselves and our doubts in brittle phrases and carefully contrived accents — to disguise our true identities, I often felt. One *Crimson* editor wrote an article which described the entire syndrome as "academic suicide."

Now Kennedy's administration had begun to harness those swirling emotions to a new kind of politics. The disarmament movement had released emotions in many of its adherents that were far stronger than anything Tocsin's technologically precise proposals could suggest. Ghoulish fantasies of imminent destruction had become almost fashionable within our small group of liberals. Sometimes we even seemed to be indulging ourselves in subtle competitions to see who was the most obsessed. Fishermen in the troubled sea of our psyches, we often exchanged yarns about our nightmares of buildings exploding, of charred victims of nuclear attacks gagging from the radiation poisoning they had suffered. But when we shared those fearful images with our elders they hinted that the pressures of academic life must be addling our brains. They would remind us that the buildings we dreamed about were always standing the next day. Our apocalyptic premonitions made no sense, they would argue. The country we were living in was the most stable on earth. Its new President promised to be one of the greatest in its history.

Those arguments sounded so reasonable that most of us continued to blame ourselves for our discontent. We believed that we were experiencing "identity crises" — the term was quite popular that year — not a first, faint realization that there were forces loose in America which would change the nation (and Harvard College) beyond recognition in just a very few years.

That spring, 1961, I flunked the examination that would have allowed me to write an honors thesis. I had studied for weeks — memorized texts as I'd done during my senior year at Choate — but I was literally unable to understand the terms of the questions we were asked. The failure confirmed my fears about my own inadequacy. So I decided to drop out of college, leave America, explore the world and myself until I was fit to graduate from Harvard.

The Making of an Un-American, 9–11

Paul Cowan's call came from political involvement, from discontent with the academic establishment, from his own feelings of inadequacy, and from the then-new herald of the call, the Peace Corps.

 Have any of these been heralds for you?

SANA HASAN

Now I had chosen. I was, of course, under no illusion that my trip to Israel would make a major contribution to peace. In the face of Phantom jets and the interests of superpowers, individual action was pathetic. But I was determined not to give in to circumstances that seemed increasingly dangerous, to views that seemed increasingly myopic. Other nations, like the French and the Germans, had fought protracted wars, but at least their citizens had spoken to each other, traveled to each other's countries, read each other's literature. The hostility of Arabs and Israelis was historically unique: It was autistic. We had not even reached the most basic level of human communication, that of finding a means to explain to each other our rage. I believed that refusing to negotiate directly with Israel was a mistake, that all our differences could be resolved through dialogue.

"Let Us Begin: A Rigorous Dialogue Between an Egyptian and an Israeli," my second appeal in the *New York Times Magazine,* this time in the form of a joint article with the Israeli writer Amos Elon, had been my way of trying to find a means. And now, I thought, what could be a more natural way to make a dent in the wall of prejudice and ignorance that separated us from each other than the simple act of braving a taboo by going to Israel as a tourist to show that Arabs and Israelis could talk? This is how I began a voyage that was planned as a six-week summer vacation—I had reserved a plane ticket for July 21 to September 5—and turned out to last nearly three years.

Enemy in the Promised Land, 17

An Egyptian student at Harvard in 1970 before the Camp David Accords between Israel and Egypt, Sana Hasan hoped that her trip to Israel would "make a dent in the wall of prejudice and ignorance."

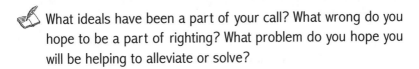 What ideals have been a part of your call? What wrong do you hope to be a part of righting? What problem do you hope you will be helping to alleviate or solve?

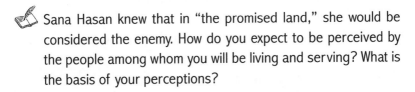 Sana Hasan knew that in "the promised land," she would be considered the enemy. How do you expect to be perceived by the people among whom you will be living and serving? What is the basis of your perceptions?

KATHLEEN NORRIS

When my husband and I moved nearly twenty years ago from New York to that house in South Dakota, only one wise friend in Manhattan understood the inner logic of the journey. Others, appalled, looked up Lemmon, South Dakota (named for G.E. "Dad" Lemmon, a cattleman and wheeler-dealer of the early 1900s, and home of the Petrified Wood Park—the world's largest—gloriously eccentric example of American folk art) in their atlases and shook their heads. How could I leave the artists' and writers' community in which I worked, the diverse and stimulating environment of a great city, for such barrenness? Had I lost my mind? But I was young, still in my twenties, an apprentice poet certain of the rightness of returning to the place where I suspected I would find my stories. As it turns out, the Plains have been essential not only for my growth as a writer, they have formed me spiritually. I would even say they have made me a human being.

St. Hilary, a fourth-century bishop (and patron saint against snake bites) once wrote, "Everything that seems empty is full of the angels of God."

Dakota: A Spiritual Geography, 11

Kathleen Norris embarked on her journey expecting to "find her stories."

 What did you expect to find?

 Do your friends understand or, like Norris's New York friends, do they assume their world is the center of the universe, from which no sane person would depart? How do they view the place you are going? Barren? Fearsome? Exciting? Paradise? Are they resistant, bored, supportive, or envious of your decision?

 What do angels represent? Can you recall other stories of myth or legend, fiction or biography, in which the hero encountered "angels in empty places?" What "angels" have you seen in "empty places" — external or internal in your life? Do you expect to find any while on your journey? What may the "empty places" be like?

SAMUEL JOHNSON

I had desired to visit the Hebrides, or Western Islands of Scotland, so long, that I scarcely remember how the wish was originally excited; and was, in the autumn of the year 1773, induced, to take the journey, by finding in Mr. Boswell a companion whose acuteness would help my inquiry, and whose gaiety of conversation and civility of manners are sufficient to counteract the inconveniences of travel in countries less hospitable than we have passed.

A Journey to the Western Islands of Scotland, 3

JAMES BOSWELL

Dr. Johnson had for many years given me hopes that we should go together, and visit the Hebrides. Martin's *Account* of those islands had impressed us with a notion that we might there contemplate a system of life almost totally different from what we had been accustomed to see; and, to find simplicity and wildness, and all the circumstances of remote time or place, so near to our native great island, was an object within the reach of reasonable curiosity. Dr. Johnson has said in his *Journey*, "that he scarcely remembered how the wish to visit the Hebrides was excited"; but he told me, in summer 1763, that his father put Martin's *Account* into his hands when he was very young, and that he was much pleased with it. We reckoned there would be some inconveniences and hardships, and perhaps a little danger; but these we were persuaded were magnified in the imagination of everybody. When I was at Ferney, in 1764, I mentioned our design to Voltaire. He looked at me, as if I had talked of going to the North Pole, and said, "You do not insist on my accompanying you?" "No, sir." "Then I am very willing you should go."

A Journal of a Tour to the Hebrides with Samuel Johnson, 4

Samuel Johnson and James Boswell are journalists beyond compare. The journals each produced from their travels together in the Outer Hebrides Islands off the western coast of Scotland are fascinating in showing how two people may have the same experience and see it differently. Johnson appears to have been called to Scotland by childhood reading. Boswell was called to Scotland by the opportunity it afforded to observe Johnson!

 What are the primary interests calling you into service-learning overseas?

Both Boswell and Johnson (in other passages) admit to a certain level of fear about the journey. Johnson alleviates his anxiety by the thought of the companionship of Boswell.

 Are you embarking on the journey with, as yet, no known friend? Are you glad to be striking out on your own? Is there anxiety for you in being alone or are you confident of making new friends?

 Are there "Voltaires" among your family and friends, happy for you to go as long as they do not have to join you?

STAGE II

PREPARING
FOR THE JOURNEY

On recognizing the call, few heroes depart instantly. Most go through a period of preparation in which they tell others of their plans, take care of matters at home, and gather belongings and information they believe will prove useful on the road. The decision to embark may be met with resistance, support, or indifference, and these reactions may engender greater resolve or indecision on the part of the hero.

In myth, legend, and fairy tale, and in the rites of passage of many cultures, the departing hero is given new equipment for the journey. It may be a precious book, an amulet to bring good fortune, a horse, or a sword with which to slay the fierce beasts. The hero is often decked in new clothing, a symbol of the task she is to perform or the person she is to become. Sometimes the new dress is ornate, befitting a leader. Sometimes it is protective, such as a heavy cape or a breastplate. Sometimes it is an article of clothing worn only by adults. Sometimes it represents, like the novice's habit, the simplicity and humility required for a time of testing. And occasionally, as in the case of the young prince who must prove himself worthy of the commoners he will one day govern, the dress for the hero's journey is a disguise.

For some departing heroes, the preparation brings only excitement and joy; for others a considerable amount of anxiety; for most a mixture of conflicting feelings. "Should I or shouldn't I?" is the common question of those preparing to depart, whether it is asked about an item to go into a suitcase or the question of whether to accept the call at all.

For some travelers, preparation includes wanting to know as much as possible in advance, while others are confident that they know enough already or else are willing and able to let the adventure ahead hold mystery. Only the experience itself will tell the traveler whether the preparation in which she engaged was helpful or whether it was excess baggage to be jettisoned at the first opportunity.

SANA HASAN

Everything seemed perfect that day. The weather was warm but not too hot. My father's mood was excellent: I was not late, and the leg of lamb was pink and juicy the way he liked it. Then I made my announcement. Not daring to look my mother or father in the eye, I informed my sister of my plans—just loud enough so my parents would be sure to overhear. They should not count on my joining them on vacation in Europe this year; I was going to Israel instead. There was silence. My mother could not have looked more shocked if I had uttered an obscenity. "Listen, my dear," she said with that afflicted tone she frequently used. "Your father may not have a great fortune because he did not steal and accept bribes like so many of his colleagues in public office, but he is bequeathing you one thing that money cannot buy—a reputation of gold. His integrity has won him the respect of past and present regimes alike. You will not bring him dishonor in his old age!" And she added icily that if I went to Israel I would be completely disowned by my family and would not be permitted to set foot in the house ever again.

In the end her tears prevailed where her threats had failed. Her argument that my father would be imprisoned on my account also helped. But I clung to my resolve to visit Israel as soon as circumstances would permit it.

Enemy in the Promised Land, 12–13

Did you try to set the stage, as did Sana Hasan, for telling parents or best friends of your decision to leave? How did you expect your parents or your friends to react to your decision? Did they at once agree with the wisdom of your choice or did you have to bring them around to your point of view?

 Did your resolve waver as the result of their response?

 Whether supportive or opposing, why do you think they reacted as they did?

MARY KINGSLEY

My attention was next turned to getting ready things to take with me. Having opened upon myself the sluice gates of advice, I rapidly became distracted. My friends and their friends alike seemed to labour under the delusion that I intended to charter a steamer and was a person of wealth beyond the dreams of avarice. The only thing to do in this state of affairs was to gratefully listen and let things drift. They showered on me various preparations of quinine and other so-called medical comforts, mustard leaves, a patent filter, a hot-water bottle, and last but not least a large square bottle purporting to be malt and cod-liver oil, which, rebelling against an African temperature, arose in its wrath, ejected its cork, and proclaimed itself an efficient but not too savoury glue.

Not only do the things you have got to take, but the things you have got to take them in, present a fine series of problems to the young traveller. Crowds of witnesses testified to the forms of baggage holders they had found invaluable, and these, it is unnecessary to say, were all different in form and material.

With all this *embarras de choix* I was too distracted to buy anything new in the way of baggage except a long waterproof sack neatly closed at the top with a bar and handle. Into this I put blankets, boots, books, in fact anything that would not go into my portmanteau or black bag. From the first I was haunted by a conviction that its bottom would come out, but it never did, and in spite of the fact that it had ideas of its own about the arrangement of its contents, it served me well throughout my voyage.

Travels in West Africa, 4–5

Packing is always part of the preparation for a journey.

 Did friends pellet you with advice?

 What did you select and what did you leave behind? Are there things you now realize you did not need, or things you wish you had brought? What do the things you chose to bring say about your expectations and your needs? What do they symbolize?

 One of the charms of Mary Kingsley's journal is her amusing way of relating the realities of travel. Were you and your luggage friends or have you wrestled all the way?

JAMES BOSWELL

From an erroneous apprehension of violence, Dr. Johnson had provided a pair of pistols, some gunpowder, and a quantity of bullets: but upon being assured we should run no risk of meeting any robbers, he left [behind] his arms and ammunition.

A Journal of a Tour to the Hebrides with Samuel Johnson, 35

Johnson gave up his pistols and ammunition apparently willingly, trusting the advice of Boswell and other Scots.

 What were you advised? Did you accept counsel readily? Do you wish now you had or had not followed the advice of friends — or program sponsors?

 Against what did you think you might need to defend yourself? What provisions did you take to aid your journey?

 What assumptions did you make that caused you to pack the unnecessary? What do you wish you had been persuaded to leave behind? Did any of your possessions cause you embarrassment in your new culture? Why?

Kathleen Norris

I want to make it clear that my move did not take me "back to the land" in the conventional sense. I did not strike out on my own to make a go of it with "an acre and a cow," as a Hungarian friend naively imagined. As the homesteaders of the early twentieth century soon found out, it is not possible to survive on even 160 acres in western Dakota. My move was one that took me deep into the meaning of inheritance, as I had to try to fit myself into a complex network of long-established relationships.

Dakota: A Spiritual Geography, 3

One of the inevitable components of preparing for departure is explaining yourself to your associates. Having chosen service-learning rather than a traditional study abroad program, you may find your friends, parents, and teachers leaping to judgments about your purpose and motives, and you may have found that their judgments are off the mark.

 What have your associates said, and how have you reacted?

 Is there, in your going, an effort to fit yourself into "a complex network of long-established relationships?" Are you in any way looking for "the meaning of inheritance?"

PAUL COWAN

Soon I went to a kibbutz, and the work I did there helped me to rid my mind of the morbid impressions I had collected in Cambridge, Massachusetts, and in London.... Sometimes I was accompanied by some of the Jews who had lived on the kibbutz for years. Our conversations covered millennia. Standing on the jetty at Caesarea, where the first of the Crusaders landed their vessels, we would talk about the guns that had been smuggled in along the Mediterranean Coast during World War II.

Such Israelis showed me something that was lacking in myself. They possessed a past they could see, a present they had created, a future they were building. None of those things belonged to me.

One day, shortly after I had left the kibbutz, I hitchhiked to Tiberias. The man who picked me up had spent all of World War II working with the Haganah to smuggle immigrants into Palestine. For hours he told me stories of his adventures, and as I compared them with my own tiny repertoire of exploits I became quite envious. Then, after nightfall, we entered the Galilee and began to drive past its rich green fields. At about nine o'clock we drew close to Mount Hermon. My new friend stopped his car. He took his young daughter by the hand and, with a flashlight to show the way beneath the Galilean sky, began to wander through the large meadow. "I have studied the flowers of Israel for years," he explained to me. "Now I know every plant that grows in my country. I feel them as part of my life. Near here is the first kibbutz I worked at. I came here from Poland, a young boy who knew nothing of crops and cultivation. Now I want to share with my child what I have learned, what my country has done."

A young man with no real home, I longed to feel that emotion, too. Israelis thought I was crazy not to accept their solution to my problem. I had only to return from the Diaspora.

"This is the only place in the world where a Jew can walk down the streets of any city without worrying that someone will make an anti-Semitic remark to him." That was the first thing an Israeli ever said to me: a gnarled, tough old Russian I met the day my ship landed in Haifa. He had encouraged me to tell him about my life in America, and I had told him about my experiences at Choate. I guess he began to see me as a potential immigrant to the homeland. He sent me to the kibbutz near Mount Carmel and kept track of me from then on. Months afterward, when I told him that I still felt my work was in the United States, he seemed hurt and angry. "You must feel the way I do, even though you're an American and nearly a *goy*. When will you learn that there's no place for us Jews out there?"

The Making of an Un-American, 13–14

Paul Cowan traveled first to Israel where he expected to feel at home. But despite the encouragement and even pressure from fellow Jews, he believed his mission lay elsewhere.

 What travel have you done before this service-learning program? How did it prepare you for this experience and in what ways?

ANTHONY WINKLER

Two nights later we pulled into Miami. Here an enclave of Jamaicans fleeing the socialist regime of Michael Manley had lately established themselves, many of them cousins and friends from my childhood days. We stopped off to see them before departing for Jamaica and were ambushed with dire prophecy about the violent end that awaited us on the island....

Everyone in the room can tell you in an instant what's to blame for the island's fallen state: The People's National Party and its garrulous leader, Prime Minister Michael Manley....

In 1972, the People's National Party finally swept into power with Michael Manley as their leader, and right away began – if the hordes of expatriate Jamaicans were to be believed – the downfall of the island. Manley announced that his government would pursue a policy of democratic socialism and instituted a series of land reform measures directed against absentee landlords. Land deemed to be "idle" was purchased by the government, paid for in bonds redeemable at a distant date, and turned over to small tenant farmers for cultivation. Squads of relief workers were organized and employed by the government to clean the streets. These "Crash Programme Workers", as they were called, were seen by well-off Jamaicans as socialist provocateurs sent into their neighbourhoods to stir up trouble. The expatriates tell of driving out of their gates and encountering knots of Crash Programme workers squatting on the shoulder of the road, glaring murderously at them.

Night after night we hear the same stories. Manley is a communist. He worships Castro. He gave money to the Rhodesian rebels. He is inciting the Jamaican poor; one day, the rabble will heed him, rise up and butcher the middle class.

These stories come from aunts and uncles and cousins and childhood friends. They sit in the living rooms of comfortable houses and tell the grim tales over and over again. Many of them have gotten their money out of the island. The signs are unmistakable: fine clothes; lavishly furnished homes; Cadillacs, Mercedes Benzes, BMWs in the driveway; jewellery dangling from the necks and ears and fingers of their wives. These Jamaicans are doctors and lawyers and dentists and managers and businessmen and veterinarians. On the island they had maids and gardeners and nannies. Their women shudder at the horror of Jamaica; their men voice outrage, anger. Some of them still have businesses on the island to which they must fly weekly: Miami is turning into a bedroom community for Jamaica.

But the poor Jamaican, you say, in defence of a government you have never lived under, a prime minister you know only through rumour, isn't Manley trying to help the poor?

"Let me tell you about the Jamaican poor," a man says sagaciously…. "You want to know why he's poor? He's poor because as long as he can flash his dick around and drink a little rum on Saturday, and play a little domino on Sunday, and once in a while a little backyard cricket, he is a happy man, content with his life. And so help me God, if Manley will just leave this brute alone, everything would be fine in Jamaica."

"Hear, hear," the roomful of exiles murmur.

"Jamaica mash up," one says.

"Jamaica finished. Over. Done," another declaims.

"Anybody who goes back to Jamaica now is a fool. A damn fool."

The eyes in the room swing accusingly at us. Cathy squirms uneasily at the stares.

Going Home to Teach, 27–32

Have you, as you prepared to depart, talked with people, read books or articles, or seen documentary or fictional movies or television programs about the country to which you are going?

 Before Anthony Winkler returned to Jamaica, he heard from middle-class Jamaicans about the evils of the leader of the political party to which most of them were opposed. What points of view are being represented to you about your chosen destination? Record these points of view as did Winkler, and in a few months reassess them in light of your experience and study.

JANE ADDAMS

It was suddenly made quite clear to me that I was lulling my conscience by a dreamer's scheme, that a mere paper reform had become a defense for continued idleness, and that I was making it a *raison d'être* for going on indefinitely with study and travel. It is easy to become the dupe of a deferred purpose, of the promise the future can never keep, and had fallen into the meanest type of self-deception in making myself believe that all this was in preparation for great things to come. Nothing less than the moral reaction following the experience at a bull-fight had been able to reveal to me that so far from following in the wake of a chariot of philanthropic fire, I had been tied to the tail of the veriest ox-cart of self-seeking.

I had made up my mind that next day, whatever happened, I would begin to carry out the plan, if only by talking about it. I can well recall the stumbling and uncertainty with which I finally set it forth to Miss Starr, my old-time school friend, who was one of our party. I even dared to hope that she might join in carrying out the plan, but nevertheless I told it in the fear of that disheartening experience which is so apt to afflict our most cherished plans when they are at last divulged, when we suddenly feel that there is nothing there to talk about, and as the golden dream slips through our fingers we are left to wonder at our own fatuous belief. But gradually the comfort of Miss Starr's companionship, the vigor and enthusiasm which she brought to bear upon it, told both in the growth of the plan and upon the sense of its validity, so that by the time we had reached the enchantment of the Alhambra, the scheme had become convincing and tangible although still most hazy in detail.

A month later we parted in Paris, Miss Starr to go back to Italy, and I to journey on to London to secure as many sugges-tions as possible from those wonderful places of which we had heard, Toynbee Hall and the People's Palace. So that it finally came about that in June, 1888, five years after my first visit in

East London, I found myself at Toynbee Hall equipped not only with a letter of introduction from Canon Fremantle, but with high expectations and a certain belief that whatever perplexities and discouragement concerning the life of the poor were in store for me, I should at least know something at first hand and have the solace of daily activity. I had confidence that although life itself might contain many difficulties, the period of mere passive receptivity had come to an end, and I had at last finished with the everlasting "preparation for life," however ill-prepared I might be.

It was not until years afterward that I came upon Tolstoy's phrase "the snare of preparation," which he insists we spread before the feet of young people, hopelessly entangling them in a curious inactivity at the very period of life when they are longing to construct the world anew and to conform it to their own ideals.

Twenty Years at Hull-House, 60–61

Those who choose service are generally idealists, with hopes and visions for a better world, and with ideas for making it so.

 What ideas and dreams have you had for "constructing the world anew?"

 Was your choice of service-learning motivated at all by restlessness with "the endless snare of preparation?"

 Have you volunteered in the past? Has it brought "the solace of daily activity?" Is there something in your life for which you need solace? In what ways do you expect your service-learning to provide for that need?

STAGE III

DEPARTING AND SEPARATING

In movies, novels, legends, and sometimes in life itself, there are the dramatic final moments before separation when the departing hero says farewell, starts on the road leading away from home, with or without the final glance backward that is supposed to tell all and predict the road he will take in the future.

The separation may not be so abrupt or melodramatic as those portrayed in the movies, and may not seem important at the time. But even a series of lighthearted good-byes marks the time of change, for when the hero is reunited with home and friends, both he and they will be different.

The soon-to-be sojourner usually anticipates with excitement the promise that lies ahead.

But departure's other face is separation, accompanied sometimes by a sense of relief and as often with a twinge or more of sadness for the past that will never be fully recovered. The hero knows that she is beginning a journey that will leave her changed, else why would she have accepted the call? Although she cannot predict the exact direction of the road to come, the hero may be sure that old ideas, habits, relationships, values, and beliefs will not remain untouched by the encounters she will have along the hero's path.

And even home will not be frozen in time and space while awaiting the hero's return, as Rip Van Winkle discovered.

EMILY BRONSON CONGER

> I, turning to my friends, said: "I am going to the Philippines;
> but do not, I beg of you, come to the dock to see me off."
> I did not then realize what it meant to start alone.
>
> *An Ohio Woman in the Philippines, 7*

"I did not then realize what it meant to start alone." The poignant words of Emily Conger as she set sail for the Philippines illustrate one of the most valuable dimensions of Partnership programs. Some students would say it is also the most difficult. Whether we travel alone or with known and trusted companions, every hero's journey is in the end a solitary one. Only the individual can face the challenges, win the battles with such beasts as doubt and loneliness, change assumptions that allow the passage through the gates and win the victories along the way. Each person must discover his own boon and chart his own course.

Surrounded as we are first with parents and family, then with peers, it is easy to imagine that we will always have the support of the group. But it is on the hero's journey to the autonomy of adulthood that we realize that there are challenges to be faced and decisions to be made that no one can make for us. The moment we embark on the journey, separating from the old sources of support, is symbolic of the road ahead.

 How do you feel about "starting alone?" Excited, eager, anxious, sad, fearful? All of the above?

Sana Hasan

Pitch Dark. The roar builds. A tiny particle detaches itself from the earth and soars up, intent on its solitary course. The voyage has begun.

This was it. I was sure of it now. There was that sharp pain in my elbows—an old, familiar symptom of fear. Up to the moment when the door of the plane closed behind me with irrevocable finality, going to Israel had been flirtation with danger: secret visits to the Israeli consulate, hushed conversations with close friends in Cambridge cafés; I knew all along that I could still back out of it—even after having obtained the visa, even after having purchased my ticket. But now I had gone too far to retreat.

A blinding flash of light slashed the sky. For some time, the airplane struggled upward, trying to hoist itself over the somber clouds. Then, as if resigned to its fate, it pitched ahead into the night. I pressed my forehead against the window, trying to pierce through the darkness outside. My eyes roamed about in search of land. There were no frontiers here, only the sky, spread out like a veil. I remembered the maps in my geography books. They were always shaded black and labeled "Occupied Palestine."

Nothing was ever said about developments on Palestinian sod since gangs of "marauders" had "stolen" it with the help of Great Britain, the United States, and other imperialist countries. Furthermore, all the pages about Israel were missing from the *World Economic Handbook* on the shelf of our school library. The same treatment was meted out to the venerable *Encyclopaedia Britannica*.

In sixth grade, our civics textbook, which bore the Arabic epigraph *"Al ilm nur"* ("Learning is light"), taught us all we needed to know on the subject of Israel. Palestine was an Arab nation that should have lived a prosperous and good life, but evil people had pounced on its land, seized its homes, and indiscriminately butchered innocent civilians.

Just in case we had missed it, our reading and poetry book reiterated the point:

> Rise in vengeance!
> Crush the heads of the marauders!
> Make out of Palestine a fatherland for the Arabs,
> And a graveyard for the Jews.

And our homework lent the subject the implacable logic of grammar:

> The following words are in the accusative. Indicate the reason for this:
>
> > We will not forget the *land* of Palestine.
> > We will expel the *usurper* from our land.
>
> The words underlined in the following sentences are in the nominative. Indicate the reason for this:
>
> > The *battle* for the sake of Palestine is a duty.
> > The *Arabs* will drive the Jews out of Palestine.

Very early on, my fear of these "evil people" turned into a forbidden attraction. I often daydreamed about crossing the Egyptian border into Israel with the same yearning nineteenth-century adventurers must have felt at the thought of exploring darkest Africa.

Enemy in the Promised Land, 3–4

Sana Hasan describes the moment when she realized there was no turning back.

 Was there a moment when you knew you had crossed the Rubicon? What were you thinking and feeling?

 Imagine a fictional or real hero whose story you know, and compare your reaction to the one you believe he or she may have had at the moment of departing.

 For Sana Hasan, Israel was "a forbidden attraction." Is there anything of the forbidden attraction in your program choice?

JANE ADDAMS

To return to my last year at school, it was inevitable that the pressure toward religious profession should increase as graduating day approached. So curious, however, are the paths of moral development that several times during subsequent experiences have I felt that this passive resistance of mine, this clinging to an individual conviction, was the best moral training I received at Rockford College. During the first decade of Hull-House, it was felt by propagandists of divers social theories that the new Settlement would be a fine coign of vantage from which to propagate social faiths, and that a mere preliminary step would be the conversion of the founders; hence I have been reasoned with hours at a time, and I recall at least three occasions when this was followed by actual prayer. In the first instance, the honest exhorter who fell upon his knees before my astonished eyes, was an advocate of single tax upon land values. He begged, in that indirect phraseology which is deemed appropriate for prayer, that "the sister might see the beneficent results it would bring to the poor who live in the awful congested districts around this very house."

Twenty Years at Hull-House, 41–42

Jane Addams describes the pressure on her to declare her religious commitment while in college. Her departure from the college to follow her own path relieved her, at least for a time, of making a decision about religion. Later, after the founding and development of Hull-House, Addams was to encounter this kind of pressure again and again as people of various convictions sought to make her one with them and their cause.

 What experiences have you had of being pressured to join, conform, or agree to a path for yourself that was charted by others? Was your decision to leave home and campus for service-learning abroad in any way a reaction of either assent to or rejection of such pressures?

 Have you learned anything about others and about yourself which may be of use to you in the future when your allegiance is being sought for ideas or behavior to which you do not want to subscribe?

ANTHONY WINKLER

It was easy to say goodbye to Southern California even after thirteen years, three degrees, two homes, six motorcars, and one marriage. Southern California is a vast motel into which people check in and out without a sense of attachment or sentimentality. Most of the people in Southern California really live elsewhere—in the heartland of the Midwest, in the ethnic neighbourhoods of eastern cities, in some small town from the deep south where their parents and siblings remained and to which they return for holidays, anniversaries, funerals, family reunions, and periodic doses of reality. Southern California is the geographic equivalent of a salesman's soul: fretful, insomniac, longing, ambitious, thwarted, and once in a while on a full mooned night, slightly demented.

I had lived here during the episodic convulsions of the flower children, the anti-war movement, the Manson family madness; through the SLA, the Black Power movement, Women's Liberation, Chairman Mao, Gay Liberation, Black Panthers, Open Enrollment, Watergate, and Pyramid Power; I had seen cause succeed cause, fad follow fad, manners of speech and gesture come and go, barbers become stylists, and haircuts shoot up overnight from $2.50 to $15. Where the land lays down no laws and traditions, there is vacuum; and where there is vacuum there is always an inrush of tormented ideology into people's minds. Southern California is a vast desert dominated by the ethics of "should." And what should be or shouldn't be depends on which ideologue is currently in vogue and which lately minted creed now reigns over the hungers and cravings of a population starving for the certainties of lost childhoods.

Going Home to Teach, 20

For Anthony Winkler the separation was easy, for he had never felt at home in the United States. He is harsh in writing about Los Angeles, but equally so in writing about his native Jamaica.

 How do you feel about leaving home and campus? What are you glad to be leaving behind? What do you think you will miss?

 What ideologies are you taking with you? Identifying these beliefs and their source may help you when you are challenged abroad by those with a different point of view. Which positions have you studied and thought out carefully, and which have you assumed simply because they are currently and locally accepted by most of your associates?

MARY KINGSLEY

It was the beginning of August '93 when I first left England for "the Coast." Preparations of quinine with postage partially paid arrived up to the last moment, and a friend hastily sent two newspaper clippings, one entitled "A Week in a Palm-oil Tub," which was supposed to describe the sort of accommodation, companions, and fauna likely to be met with on a steamer going to West Africa, and on which I was to spend seven to *The Graphic* contributor's one; the other from *The Daily Telegraph,* reviewing a French book of "Phrases in common use" in Dahomey. The opening sentence in the latter was, "Help, I am drowning." Then came the inquiry, "If a man is not a thief?" and then another cry, "The boat is upset." "Get up, you lazy scamps," is the next exclamation, followed almost immediately by the question, "Why has not this man been buried?" "It is fetish that has killed him, and he must lie here exposed with nothing on him until only the bones remain," is the cheerful answer. This sounded discouraging to a person whose occupation would necessitate going about considerably in boats, and whose fixed desire was to study fetish. So with a feeling of foreboding gloom I left London for Liverpool — none the more cheerful for the matter-of-fact manner in which the steamboat agents had informed me that they did not issue return tickets by the West African lines of steamers.

Travels in West Africa, 5

Mary Kingsley relates her feelings upon departure as "foreboding gloom," but she does it so cheerfully and amusingly that one wonders if she really took the warnings seriously. Or perhaps her wit and good humor came only after she returned safely to England.

 What did you experience upon departure? Excitement? Pleasure? Anxiety? Who along the way created, intensified or modifed your feelings?

Langston Hughes

Melodramatic maybe, it seems to me now. But then it was like throwing a million bricks out of my heart when I threw the books into the water. I leaned over the rail of the S.S. *Malone* and threw the books as far as I could out into the sea — all the books I had had at Columbia, and all the books I had lately bought to read.

The books went down into the moving water in the dark off Sandy Hook. Then I straightened up, turned my face to the wind, and took a deep breath. I was a seaman going to sea for the first time — a seaman on a big merchant ship. And I felt that nothing would ever happen to me again that I didn't want to happen. I felt grown, a man, inside and out. Twenty-one.

I was twenty-one.

Four bells sounded. As I stood there, whiffs of salt spray blew in my face. The afterdeck was deserted. The big hatches were covered with canvas. The booms were all tied up to the masts, and the winches silent. It was dark. The old freighter, smelling of crude oil and garbage, engines pounding, rolled through the pitch-black night. I looked down on deck and noticed that one of my books had fallen into the scupper. The last book. I picked it up and threw it far over the rail into the water below, that was too black to see. The wind caught the book and ruffled its pages quickly, then let it fall into the rolling darkness. I think it was a book by H. L. Mencken.

You see, books had been happening to me. Now the books were cast off back there somewhere in the chum of spray and night behind the propeller. I was glad they were gone.

The Big Sea, 3–4

Langston Hughes's act was indeed most dramatic, symbolizing his casting off of Columbia University and New York and the ideas that had dominated his thinking and his life there.

 What books did you sell, or pack away, or bring with you? What do these books represent in your hopes for the adventure ahead?

 Hughes says that "books had been happening to me." What does he mean by this phrase? Have you had similar thoughts and feelings about school and study?

 Hughes also relates feeling "grown, a man, inside and out." Are you thinking differently of yourself now that you have embarked?

KATHLEEN NORRIS

I've never thought of myself as an ascetic. In fact, one of my best friends has said that denying myself was never what got me in trouble. But in acclimating myself to the bareness of the Plains after the cornucopia of New York City I found to my surprise that not only did I not lament the loss of urban stimulation, but I began to seek out even more deprivation than my isolated prairie town of 1,600 could provide. I gave up watching television, except for the Miss America Pageant and the Academy Awards (the former because there's always the chance that the talent competition will include a baton twirler or a ventriloquist, or, better yet, a baton-twirling ventriloquist; the latter because, though I've mostly given up movies as well, once a year I like to see what people in Hollywood are wearing).

As living on the Plains has nudged me into a quieter life, I've discovered that this is what I wanted. I've had to read more, and more widely, so as not to become provincial, but interlibrary loans take care of me here. Reading is a solitary act, one in keeping with the silence of the Plains, but it's also paradoxically public, as it deepens my connections with the larger world.

The silence of the Plains, this great unpeopled landscape of earth and sky, is…an unfathomable silence that has the power to reform you. And the Plains have changed me. I was a New Yorker for nearly six years and still love to visit my friends in the city. But now I am conscious of carrying a Plains silence within me into cities, and of carrying my city experiences back to the Plains so that they may be absorbed again back into silence, the fruitful silence that produces poems and essays.

Dakota: A Spiritual Geography, 14–15

A radical change of setting often uncovers for those who make such a change new dimensions of their personality and character. The shy discover that they are outgoing; the fearful become brave — or vice versa. Norris discovered her asceticism when she separated herself from the city and its fast-paced life.

 What has the separation from friends, family, school, and a familiar way of life revealed to you about yourself?

 Norris describes how she takes the culture of her past, the city, to be absorbed into the silence of the Plains. What have you done with the culture of home? Have you thought about it often, been homesick, stayed in close touch through the telephone or E-mail? Or have you let go of it for the time being, focusing on the new situation and its challenges?

PAUL COWAN

James Meredith was shot the day before we were supposed to leave for Guayaquil.

Throughout the evening the Associated Press reported that he'd been murdered, and those bulletins added urgency to the questions Rachel and I had been asking one another since the beginning of training. How could we work for something called a Peace Corps when there was virtual civil war at home?

Within a few hours the crisis seemed to ease. The eleven-o'clock news reported that Meredith's wounds were superficial and that leaders of all the civil-rights organizations in the country were flying to his hospital in Memphis, where they would unite to organize a mass march along the route he had mapped for himself. Perhaps, we thought on that nervous night, the sniper's bullet had really been a good-luck charm. Soon the movement would come together again.

But we wouldn't be around to witness the process. The question we had asked one another was just part of an elaborate ritual, designed to prove that we were still more radical and open-minded than the organization we had joined. But we had been seized by the rhythm of the new adventure and were eager to learn the lessons it would teach. It was too late to withdraw.

I never felt so close to the other trainees as I did that night, flying toward Guayaquil on our Braniff jet. A soldier heading for Vietnam must feel that way too; suddenly, briefly, the people with whom he might die seem his only friends, the only family he has in the world. The war is one thing, horrible; one's platoon is another thing altogether, beloved.

Nine members of our original group had been deselected or had quit; for the twenty of us who remained the act of crossing continents seemed irrevocable. Nobody had very much confidence in himself that night, or in our special project either. As we traveled from New York to Miami, to the shocking heat

76

of Panama, and then on through the tropical sunrise to Guayaquil, each of us was trying to wrest firm pledges, almost blood pledges, from our peers. "You really will leave if you don't like it, Nick?" Rachel asked. "I mean the worst thing would be to stay around for two years on an assignment that didn't make any sense." Most of the voices that murmured in the darkened cabin were posing the same tense question.

The Making of an Un-American, 171–172

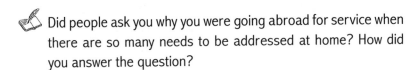

Did people ask you why you were going abroad for service when there are so many needs to be addressed at home? How did you answer the question?

How did you feel about the people on the plane also traveling to your destination, or about the other students in the program? Who seemed like a companion and who a stranger?

What pledge have you made to yourself about the service and the program? Do you have any ideas about how you will determine whether your project "makes sense?" Do you expect to trust the agency and the program director or, like Paul Cowan, are you questioning the wisdom of those who arranged the program and selected you for participation?

STAGE IV

CROSSING THE FIRST THRESHOLD

Once the separation has been effected and the journey begun in earnest, a frequent first response is exhilaration. New sights, sounds, smells, and tastes stimulate the hero's senses, just as they did for Marco Polo when he arrived in Kublai Khan's great city of Cambaluc (modern Beijing). In legend, crossing the first threshold is often pictured as entry into a mythical shining city on a hill, full of wondrous bazaars and magical inventions, of wealth, power, and promise. The newly-arrived traveler wanders through the streets, amazed at the possibilities before him.

There is a glorious freedom, a kind of "entrance into the zone of magnified power" which excites body and spirit. [9] The familiar horizon, with all of its restrictions, has been outgrown. Here are new worlds to conquer.

Accompanying responses to the initial exhilaration may be delight, wonder, joy, surprise, but also apprehension, disgust, disappointment, or confusion. These contradictory feelings may come at the same time or in any successive order.

In these early days of the journey, when the hero has crossed the threshold into what will be a new home, the stimuli come so thick and fast that he hardly knows where to focus attention — out of the bus window or on new companions? On the geography, or the people? On the new experiences, or his reactions to them?

Those who have studied the experience of strangers in a foreign land tell us that this period may last briefly or for several weeks, and is proportional to the length of time of the anticipated journey.

ANTHONY WINKLER

"Everyone going, and you coming."

So my brother greets us at the airport.

We are immersed in a throng that has just deplaned, and all around us in the cavernous terminal are piles of luggage, boxes, cartons, attended by a milling crowd of passengers. My brother isn't supposed to be in the customs hall, but he has an influential friend. The customs officials, wearing the hardened look of the bored — the trademark expression of West Indian civil servants — are pawing through open suitcases, filling out declaration forms, and levying fines as the mood takes them. Here and there passengers bicker with a customs officer, and sometimes a peal of derisive laughter rings through the room as bystanders react to one of the many raging debates.

"Me is a sufferer," a man bellows. "Me have ten pickney. De radio is for me Mumma. Her heart bad. De doctor say de radio cool her nerves."

"You still must pay duty 'pon it," the official says stonily.

"Lawd God, man!" the passenger's voice rises in outrage. "Why you must be so wicked, man? Why you want to step 'pon de head of a poor sufferer? You don't know times changing in Jamaica, man! Negar man can't take any more suffering — him heart sick wid pain and suffering."

Laughter rustles in the wake of his tirade.

The enormous crowd smells of perfume, sweat, and humus. It is a sweltering night, the air heavy and sweet with humidity, the pungent tang of kerosene fuel, the fragrance of the ocean.

Only minutes ago we were flying on the edge of a menacing blackness with nothing visible through the window except the frail light on the wing-tip of the jet and occasionally, illumined by a distant flash of lightning, shoals of dark thunderheads on the horizon. Then the plane began its descent. We knifed through a black cloud, the plane rattled and shook, and suddenly far below we saw lights that marked the presence of an invisible land.

"Jamaica," I whispered to Cathy, pointing to a light so tiny and wavering that it could have been the illumination of a lost firefly.

She squeezed my hand with excitement as the plane shuddered.

The line we now stand in snakes raggedly across the terminal, its head nudging the inspection station manned by a slouching customs officer. Voices jabber in a mixture of Jamaican patois and English. Conveyor belts rumble into the room, bearing fresh loads of cardboard boxes and battered suitcases.

The faces in the room are black, brown, swarthy, some glinting with the yellow glow of the Oriental, some an indescribable stew of races—a jumble of delicate cheekbones, puffy negroid lips, and glinting green eyes. Long dead Englishmen peer out of coal black faces; former slaves smoulder under the yellowish skins of mulattoes; an East Indian ancestor lies mummified inside the body of the half-Chinese lady resignedly waiting her turn to battle customs. "Out of Many, One People," is the Jamaican motto.

My eyes are drawn to the familiar gestures of the crowd. I see a woman to my right "cut her eyes" at a man who has ogled her. She rolls them in the corners of their sockets in a familiar Jamaican gesture and the man quails at this wordless reproof and looks long and hard at his shoes. I hear another woman kiss her teeth—making that sibilant hissing sound with her lips which, for Jamaicans, signals inexpressible contempt. When I lived in America, I couldn't use these gestures. My mind was imprisoned in conventional speech.

The crowd is peculiarly Jamaican. In America crowds are geometric things: they form straight, disciplined lines; they have shape and order like a fishbone. In Jamaica a crowd is living tissue. It throbs, stinks, and bleeds all over a room. There is no containing it in mere geometry; it will not suffer conduits or levees or postural correctness. The English for years railed against the Jamaican habit of slouching in public places, and so here and there in the throng you can see vestiges of their teachings: a grim, stout black man who shuns a nearby post, stands obdurately straight, and disdainfully eyes the horde of leaners and saggers surrounding him.

It is all here in this airport. Three hundred years of colonialism: a people who were brought here as slaves or came as plunderers, who grew into nationhood simultaneously clinging to the passive resistance mentality of the enslaved while unconsciously admiring and aping the ways of the English master, who resent and despise authority of all kinds and make a national sport of constantly haggling with it; a people mixed and hybridized in every conceivable way—racially, culturally, linguistically, spiritually—and to whom life has been so capricious and unfair that they have come over the centuries to see it as the stuff of makeshift drama.

"Lawd God Almighty, tell me who more wicked dan a Jamaica brown man? Who on dis earth more wicked and hard dan a Jamaica brown man?" a woman shrieks, as she unknots the corner of her handkerchief in which she had tied money that she must now pay out for duty.

The customs official, a brown man with a stubborn expression pasted on his face, is aloof to her shrieking and impassively continues to fill in his quadruplicate forms. The crowd chuckles at the woman's fulminations.

"Is true," a voice assents. "Brown man is de hardest man God ever put 'pon dis earth."

"Gimme a white man any day," another concurs, "no matter how him wicked, for him can't be any more wicked dan brown man."

It is the beginning of Greek chorusing that will surge through the crowd for a few minutes.

Beside me, Cathy looks bewildered, afraid.

"Everybody in Jamaica leaving, and you coming," my brother repeats gloomily.

Going Home to Teach, 33–35

Anthony Winkler was a native Jamaican, his companion Cathy was not. Upon arrival in Kingston, he interpreted and understood what was happening in the airport. She was bewildered and even a little afraid.

 Describe the scene that greeted you upon your arrival in the airport and recount the behavior you observed. What bewildered, delighted, interested, amused, or frightened you?

 "It is all here in this airport." As you learn more about the country and people to which you have come, return to this description and use it to illustrate the history and culture about which you are learning.

Emily Bronson Conger

The city seemed like one vast tropical garden, with its waving palms, gorgeous foliage and flowers, gaily colored birds and spicy odors, but mingled with the floral fragrance were other odors that betokened a foreign population.

It was my first experience in seeing all sorts and conditions of people mingling together — Chinese, Japanese, Hawaiians, English, Germans and Americans. Then the manner of dress seemed so strange, especially for the women; they wore a garment they call halicoes like the Mother Hubbard that we so much deride.

It was still early morning when my friends with a pair of fine horses drove from the shore level by winding roads up through the foot hills, ever up and up above the luxuriant groves of banana and cocoanut, the view widening, and the masses of rich foliage growing denser below or broadening into the wide sugar plantations that surrounded palatial homes. We returned for luncheon and I noted that not one house had a chimney, that every house was protected with mosquito netting; porches, doors, windows, beds, all carefully veiled.

After dinner we again set forth with a pair of fresh horses and drove for miles along the coast, visiting some of the beautiful places that we had already seen from the heights. The beauty of gardens, vines, flowers, grasses, hills, shores, ocean was bewildering. In the city itself are a thousand objects of interest, of which not the least is the market.

I had never seen tropical fish before, and was somewhat surprised by the curious shapes and varied colors of the hundreds and thousands of fish exposed for sale. I do not think there was a single color scheme that was not carried out in that harvest of the sea. Fruits and flowers were there, too, in heaps and masses at prices absurdly low. With the chatter of the natives and the shrill cry of the fishermen as they came in with their heavily laden boats, the scene was one never to be forgotten.

An Ohio Woman in the Philippines, 8–10

Emily Conger proved from the beginning that she was a keen observer. Although later she expresses freely her opinions and interpretations, in the initial days she wisely refrains, even to the point of making no speculation on why the houses had no chimneys and why they were wrapped in mosquito netting.

 What fascinated you the most in your first days?

 What was a brand-new sight, sound, taste, or smell for you?

OCTAVIO PAZ

Although I have written more than I originally intended, I have touched on only a few historical and political matters. These are questions that concern us all, and couldn't be avoided. But I would have preferred to write about what I love and feel: India did not enter me through my mind but through my senses. I have spoken of my arrival in Bombay, one morning forty years ago: I can still breathe that humid air, see and hear the crowds in the streets, remember the brilliant colors of the saris, the murmur of voices, my dazzlement before the Trimurti in Elephanta. I have also mentioned in passing the food; from it I gained, early on, a small insight that taught me more about India than a monograph.

In Light of India, 137

You need not feel compelled to interpret at this stage of the journey. In fact, it is wise to withhold judgment until you know and understand more.

 As you crossed the first threshold of your journey, what did you see, hear, taste, feel, and smell that began to introduce you to the host culture? What did you relish and what did you find distasteful?

 Make a list of every adjective that may be applied to your first observations and then write an accurate, specific, and lively description of your first impressions.

Kathleen Norris

Hospitality is of primary importance in the desert. Bedouin hospitality is legendary, as is that of the Benedictines, who are instructed by Saint Benedict in his *Rule* to "receive all guests as Christ." The people of the Great Plains can be hospitable as well, in the fashion of people who have little and are willing to share what they have. The poorest among us, in the Native American community, are exceptional in this regard, with a tradition of hospitality that has deep cultural roots in the giveaway, a sacred event that in application served the purpose of providing for the entire tribe. Hunters brought their surplus meat or buffalo robes, and those too old or infirm to hunt brought handcrafted items like quillwork; and in the exchange everyone received what was needed to survive the winter. Even today the ceremonial giveaway, in the words of Arthur Amiotte, a Lakota artist, remains an important and "reciprocal activity in which we are reminded of sacred principles," an act of giving which "ennobles the human spirit."

Visitors from urban areas are often surprised by the easy friendliness they encounter on the Plains. Even in Bismarck-Mandan (at 64,000, a major urban area by Dakota standards) strangers greet travelers on the street and welcome them warmly. Recently a motel manager drove a woman nearly two hundred miles to the town where her husband had fallen ill, and stayed with her until family arrived. This could happen in a larger city, of course, but it's the expected thing on the Plains. Like all desert hospitality, this is in part a response to the severity of the climate; here, more demonstrably than in many other places, we need each other to survive.

Dakota: A Spiritual Geography, 112–113

Although not of course always, hospitality is often the first characteristic to be noticed by the newly-arrived. Perhaps we see it because we are so anxiously looking for and needing it!

 Who welcomed you, and in what ways? How have you responded? Have you trusted the sincerity of motives or has the welcome made you somehow uneasy?

 Norris attributes the hospitality of the Great Plains to the severity of the climate. "We need each other to survive." What reasons have the local people given, or have you deduced, for the hospitality you have encountered? How does the hospitality you received compare to that given to strangers in your home culture?

JANE ADDAMS

One of the most poignant of these experiences, which occurred during the first few months after our landing upon the other side of the Atlantic, was on a Saturday night, when I received an ineradicable impression of the wretchedness of East London, and also saw for the first time the overcrowded quarters of a great city at midnight. A small party of tourists were taken to the East End by a city missionary to witness the Saturday night sale of decaying vegetables and fruit, which, owing to the Sunday laws in London, could not be sold until Monday, and, as they were beyond safe keeping, were disposed of at auction as late as possible on Saturday night. On Mile End Road, from the top of an omnibus which paused at the end of a dingy street lighted by only occasional flares of gas, we saw two huge masses of ill-clad people clamoring around two hucksters' carts. They were bidding their farthings and ha'pennies for a vegetable held up by the auctioneer, which he at last scornfully flung, with a gibe for its cheapness, to the successful bidder. In the momentary pause only one man detached himself from the groups. He had bidden in a cabbage, and when it struck his hand, he instantly sat down on the curb, tore it with his teeth, and hastily devoured it, unwashed and uncooked as it was. He and his fellows were types of the "submerged tenth," as our missionary guide told us, with some little satisfaction in the then new phrase, and he further added that so many of them could scarcely be seen in one spot save at this Saturday night auction, the desire for cheap food being apparently the one thing which could move them simultaneously. They were huddled into ill-fitting, cast-off clothing, the ragged finery which one sees only in East London. Their pale faces were dominated by that most unlovely of human expressions, the cunning and shrewdness of the bargain-hunter who starves if he cannot make a successful trade, and yet the final impression was not of ragged, tawdry clothing nor of pinched and sallow faces, but of myriads of hands, empty, pathetic, nerveless and workworn, showing white in the uncertain light of the street, and clutching forward for food which was already unfit to eat.

Perhaps nothing is so fraught with significance as the human hand, this oldest tool with which man has dug his way from savagery, and with which he is constantly groping forward. I have never since been able to see a number of hands held upward, even when they are moving rhythmically in a calisthenic exercise, or when they belong to a class of chubby children who wave them in eager response to a teacher's query, without a certain revival of this memory, a clutching at the heart reminiscent of the despair and resentment which seized me then.

Twenty Years at Hull-House, 49–50

 Recount the scene in which you first saw need in the community in which you are serving. Is there for you, as there was for Addams, a "snapshot" which you believe will stay with you always?

MARY KINGSLEY

I will not go into the details of that voyage here, much as I am given to discursiveness. They are more amusing than instructive, for on my first voyage out I did not know the Coast, and the Coast did not know me, and we mutually terrified each other. I fully expected to get killed by the local nobility and gentry; they thought I was connected with the World's Women's Temperance Association, and collecting shocking details for subsequent magic-lantern lectures on the liquor traffic; so fearful misunderstandings arose, but we gradually educated each other, and I had the best of the affair; for all I had got to teach them was that I was only a beetle and fetish hunter, and so forth, while they had to teach me a new world, and a very fascinating course of study I found it. And whatever the Coast may have to say against me — for my continual desire for hair-pins, and other pins, my intolerable habit of getting into water, the abominations full of ants, that I brought into their houses, or things emitting at unexpectedly short notice vivid and awful stenches — they cannot but say that I was a diligent pupil, who honestly tried to learn the lessons they taught me so kindly, though some of those lessons were hard to a person who had never previously been even in a tame bit of tropics, and whose life for many years had been an entirely domestic one in a University town.

Travels in West Africa, 5–6

Kingsley leads us to expect that she will say that she feared death at the hands of natives, then disarmingly suggests her danger was from her own countrymen who thought she was there to condemn their drinking habits!

 In your first few days, has anyone misunderstood you and your purpose for being in the country? Was it a native or perhaps, as for Kingsley, someone from home? What was the process for you and your hosts in getting acquainted with one another?

 Mary Kingsley needed hair pins. What did you ask for in the first few days that perplexed, amused, or annoyed your hosts?

SANA HASAN

Tel Aviv was a surprise. I had always thought of Israel as a marvel of Western technology, not just because of its military might, but also because Amos Perlmutter, an Israeli professor who had visited Harvard, had told me it was "definitely part of Europe." In his view, at the root of the Middle Eastern conflict lay a clash between Western and Arab cultures. This only confirmed what I had been taught as a child: The Zionists of Palestine were an alien, *European* element, "a thorn in the heart of the Arab nation." Given all this, I had expected a grand metropolis, the gleaming jewel of Israeli dominion and efficiency. Instead, Tel Aviv resembled a Middle Eastern bazaar.

Central Station, where the *sherut* dropped me off, had regulations of its own: Pedestrians, buses, horse carriages laden with fruits, bicycles, trucks, cabs — all had right of way. Masses of people zigzagged between cars. Buses suddenly zeroed in from side alleys. Taxis pulled up in the middle of the street without warning to let off their passengers.

Vendors crowded the sidewalks. A huckster selling ice cream ran among a throng of soldiers in a queue — older soldiers, perhaps reserve officers, red-eyed, unshaven, pot-bellied under sloppy shirts, and youngsters who seemed to be returning from furlough, with short haircuts, freshly polished shoes, and pressed uniforms. Another peddler, seated at the edge of a bathtub planted in the middle of the sidewalk, was hawking toilets, sinks, gravestones, tiles from Italy, and a needlepoint portrait of Moshe Dayan. Next to a butcher's stall with the fanciful name "Le Coq d'Or — kosher" was a stand with all kinds of bagels. The grocer, wearing a sweaty red T-shirt and flashing a gold canine tooth when he smiled, held out a steaming ear of corn and asked me if I was an American tourist and would I go dancing with him that night.

Architecturally, Tel Aviv was a nightmare. In lieu of the streamlined terminals, gleaming skyscrapers, stately mansions, and elegant parks with statues and lush fountains I had imagined, it was a town of four-story cubes. The drab brick buildings, with their unwashed slate-colored windows and walls corroded by pollution and the salty sea breeze, lent it the atmosphere of a shabby provincial town....

I had imagined the Israeli equivalent of the Pyramids to resemble the Champs Elysées. To my surprise, it turned out to be much like any other street in Tel Aviv, except that its entire length was devoted to the junk-food business. I walked past pizzerias displaying stale, triangular slices and synthetic juices bubbling in transparent plastic tubs — the choice was between a greenish mauve and a greenish yellow. Farther on, a seedy little restaurant spilled out into the street, its window featuring stacks of greasy chicken and cold, soggy french fries. Beside it, on the sidewalk, gray slabs of meat were being cooked beyond redemption.

Enemy in the Promised Land, 39–41

 Describe what you expected to find in your new surrounding and what you in fact found. What was the source of your expectations?

 It is possible that after a few weeks or months you will see your new land and its geography differently from your first impressions. Save a blank page here to add your changed perspective as you near the end of your journey.

PAUL COWAN

From the day we arrived at training, our field experience in Ciudad Juárez had been described as the *summa* of our special program. We would live with poor Mexicans and observe their relations to the city government and to local self-help organizations. The month-long experience would help us synthesize all of the lessons about community development we'd learned in Albuquerque and provide a dress rehearsal for our years in Guayaquil.

By the time we were actually supposed to leave for Juárez, the Peace Corps bureaucracy had developed a guilty fear that the Mexican government would cause an international incident if it discovered that a bunch of trainees were living on its soil. Those people had so much pride, we were told by our superiors, that they refused to cooperate with the Peace Corps in any way. It was the Latin *macho* complex, a pride that amounted almost to paranoia: to associate with a foreign organization like ours would be to make a public admission of their inability to help themselves.

So the training-center staff provided us a cover. We were told to pose as a group of graduate students from the University of New Mexico who had been assigned to live with the poorest people in Juárez in order to study the Spanish language and Mexican culture.

They couldn't have invented a more ridiculous disguise. The few people in the *colonias* who could imagine that a university student might get credit for spending time away from both his campus and his country were even more suspicious of us than the majority of Mexicans we met, to whom no set of words would explain why a group of North Americans would want to cross the border and spend time with them. What kind of people would live in the *colonias* to learn the Spanish language? The sophisticates connected us to the FBI, the CIA, the Border Patrol. Most people just thought we were crazy.

The fact that we were forbidden to reveal our identities gave us a peculiarly suspicious sense of ourselves: there must be something shameful about an identity which has to be hidden. The emotions instilled in us so carelessly, would persist for two years, alienating the most conformist, most conventionally ambitious members of our group from the organization they had wanted to serve.

It turned out that the precautions were unnecessary. A week before we left Juárez one of the trip's codirectors told an El Paso television announcer that a Peace Corps project was training in the area. Apparently, he didn't realize that television signals can cross borders without passports: when the item was carried on the evening newscast it was seen in both El Paso and Juárez. The Mexicans realized what we were doing in their city, and for a day the Peace Corps was panicked. But soon it became clear that no one in Juárez, except the silly gringos who administered us, cared enough about us to ask us to stay or to leave.

When we got back to Albuquerque we learned that Peace Corps groups had been training in Mexico for years. The training-center staff, the desk officers in Washington, hadn't been efficient enough to ask the simple question of some coworkers that would uncover that fact. So they built a castle of fear from their false information.

For most of the month Rachel and I were able to maintain some distance from the Peace Corps staff. We were far more interested in Colonia Emiliano Zapata, where we lived, than in the organization that had deposited us there. The people we were staying with were so kind, so generous that despite their confusion about our role in the community they allowed us to enter freely into their lives.

It was the richest experience I had enjoyed in years. For the first time since I left Chestertown I felt as if I was part of a new, exciting culture, not of a movement composed of my peers whose avowed intent was to change a way of life it barely understood. And I lost some of my left-wing preconceptions as I realized that the America I was beginning to despise still seemed the land of promise to many of my Mexican neighbors, would seem a land of promise to many poor Ecuadorians, as Rudolfo Benitez had said. My disappointment in my country became a far more complicated emotion.

The Making of an Un-American, 141–143

The first days and even weeks in another country or culture can be filled with miscalculations and misperceptions on the part of both guest and host. Paul Cowan's first days were made more difficult by the supervisor's instructions to conceal his true identity. While few visitors conceal in such a deliberate way, we sometimes fail to be truthful out of concern for the host or for our own image. For example, we may say that we understand something when in fact we do not.

 Did you have such an experience? What was the result?

Cowan reports the importance of these training days in Mexico as a means of shedding preconceptions and learning firsthand about the attitudes of the Mexicans. He also admits that what the U.S. Peace Corps supervisors thought would be important to the Mexicans turned out to be a matter of indifference to most Mexicans.

 What preconceptions have you begun to shed?

Cowan discovered that his hosts, the Mexicans, were kind, generous, and welcoming even while confused about his purpose in being in Mexico.

 Have you had a similar experience?

LANGSTON HUGHES

When we got to Teneriffe, in the Canary Islands, it was mid-afternoon and very bright. The Canaries looked like fairy islands, all sharp peaks of red rock and bright sandy beaches and little green fields dropped like patchwork between the beaches and the rocks, with the sea making a blue-white fringe around.

The Captain let us draw money — so Las Palmas seemed a gay city indeed. Ashore, three or four of us, including Ernesto and a Norwegian boy named Sven, had supper at a place with very bright lights, where they served huge platters of delicious mixed fish with big bottles of cool, white wine. Then we all went to a white villa by the sea, called *El Palacio de Amor* and stayed all night. In the morning very early, when the sun was just coming up, we drove back to the wharf in an open carriage. We kept thinking about the girls, who were Spanish, and very young and pretty. And Sven said he would like to take one of them with him.

But all those days I was waiting anxiously to see Africa. And finally, when I saw the dust-green hills in the sunlight, something took hold of me inside. My Africa, Motherland of the Negro peoples! And me a Negro! Africa! The real thing, to be touched and seen, not merely read about in a book.

That first morning when we sighted the coast, I kept leaving my work to lean over the rail and look at Africa, dim and far away, off on the horizon in a haze of light, then gradually nearer and nearer, until you could see the color of the foliage on the trees.

We put in at the port of Dakar. There were lots of Frenchmen, and tall black Senegalese soldiers in red fezes, and Mohammedans in robes, so that at first you couldn't tell if the Mohammedans were men or women.

The next day we moved on. And farther down the coast it was more like the Africa I had dreamed about — wild and palm trees tall, the sun bright, and the rivers deep. The great Africa of my dreams!

But there was one thing that hurt me a lot when I talked with the people. The Africans looked at me and would not believe I was a Negro.

You see, unfortunately, I am not black.

The Big Sea, 10

Heritage seekers have a special journey that, like adoptees seeking natural parents, may bring joy or disappointment. Our expectations never quite match reality. Not only do we have expectations about the land from which our ancestors came but also expectations about how we will be perceived and received. Most who are seeking roots look forward to special hospitality and welcome, an experience which may or may not happen.

 Are you seeking your roots? What were your expectations? What has been your experience?

STAGE V

TAKING UP THE CHALLENGES

In classic fairy tales that follow the story line of the hero's journey, a prince, often the youngest and apparently weakest, is faced with three, five, seven, twelve, or thirteen challenges, each successively harder. Like Hercules, who took on twelve labors, the prince must accept and accomplish the tasks before him if he is to win the hand of the beautiful princess and be named heir to the throne. The tasks require bravery and resolve, but also intellect and imagination. Although some heroes try to pass on the challenge to someone else, in the end they must either take up the gauntlet for themselves or lose the opportu-nity to win the prize.

In the hero's story, prior competitors have failed because of limited vision and because they have seen the tests as requiring merely strength. Like young David, who slew Goliath the Giant by means of a slingshot rather than sword and spear, the successful hero looks at the problems and puzzles before him through a new lens and approaches the seemingly impossible tasks in new ways.

In the excerpts that follow, you will see travelers who do and do not see anew. Some began their journey with images and opinions that they were later able to discard in favor of new perspectives. Others, like the unsuccessful suitor, are locked into a narrow way of seeing.

This stage in the journey deals with the challenge of understanding a new culture—its geography and natural features, its human culture and the institutions of its society. The challenges also include issues of individual relationships. Through your mind's eye, "walk around" each experience to see it from as many vantages as possible.

Put yourself in the picture, for you are no mere observer but an active player in the tale. As you gain new perspectives on the world you will make new discoveries about yourself. The hero who accepts the challenges is seen differently by the people who surround her. You will recognize the perceptions of others and, as you face into the tasks, you will have a changed notion of yourself.

KATHLEEN NORRIS

More Americans than ever, well over 70 percent, now live in urban areas and tend to see Plains land as empty. What they really mean is devoid of human presence. Most visitors to Dakota travel on interstate highways that will take them as quickly as possible through the region, past our larger cities to such attractions as the Badlands and the Black Hills. Looking at the expanse of land in between, they may wonder why a person would choose to live in such a barren place, let alone love it. But mostly they are bored: they turn up the car stereo, count the miles to civilization, and look away.

Dakota is a painful reminder of human limits, just as cities and shopping malls are attempts to deny them. This book is an invitation to a land of little rain and few trees, dry summer winds and harsh winters, a land rich in grass and sky and surprises.

The high plains, the beginning of the desert West, often act as a crucible for those who inhabit them. Like Jacob's angel, the region requires that you wrestle with it before it bestows a blessing. This can mean driving through a snowstorm on icy roads, wondering whether you'll have to pull over and spend the night in your car, only to emerge under tag ends of clouds into a clear sky blazing with stars. Suddenly you know what you're seeing: the earth has turned to face the center of the galaxy, and many more stars are visible than the ones we usually see on our wing of the spiral.

Or a vivid double rainbow marches to the east, following the wild summer storm that nearly blew you off the road. The storm sky is gunmetal gray, but to the west the sky is peach streaked with crimson. The land and sky of the West often fill what Thoreau termed our "need to witness our limits transgressed." Nature, in Dakota, can indeed be an experience of the holy.

Dakota: A Spiritual Geography, 1–2

How have the people who inhabit your host country been challenged by the land and climate? What various, and possibly contradictory, human qualities have the land and the climate shaped?

 How have you been challenged by the geography of your host land? Have you had to "wrestle" with your new location? What has it taught you?

 What "blessings" has the wrestling bestowed? Have your seen your "limits transgressed?"

MARY KINGSLEY

I inquired of all my friends as a beginning what they knew of West Africa. The majority knew nothing. A percentage said, "Oh, you can't possibly go there; that's where Sierra Leone is, the white man's grave, you know." If these were pressed further, one occasionally found that they had had relations who had gone out there after having been "sad trials," but, on consideration of their having left not only West Africa, but this world, were now forgiven and forgotten. One lady however kindly remembered a case of a gentleman who had resided some few years at Fernando Po, but when he returned an aged wreck of forty he shook so violently with ague as to dislodge a chandelier, thereby destroying a valuable tea-service and flattening the silver teapot in its midst.

No; there was no doubt about it, the place was not healthy, and although I had not been "a sad trial," yet neither had the chandelier-dislodging Fernando Po gentleman. So I next turned my attention to cross-examining the doctors. "Deadliest spot on earth," they said cheerfully, and showed me maps of the geographical distribution of disease. Now I do not say that a country looks inviting when it is coloured in Scheele's green or a bilious yellow, but these colours may arise from lack of artistic gift in the cartographer. There is no mistaking what he means by black, however, and black you'll find they colour West Africa from above Sierra Leone to below the Congo. "I wouldn't go there if I were you," said my medical friends, "you'll catch something; but if you must go, and you're as obstinate as a mule, just bring me — " and then followed a list of commissions from here to New York, any one of which — but I only found that out afterwards.

All my informants referred me to the missionaries. "There were," they said, in an airy way, "lots of them down there, and had been for years." So to missionary literature I addressed myself with great ardour; alas! only to find that these good people wrote their reports not to tell you how the country they resided in was, but how it was getting on towards being what it ought to be.

Travels in West Africa, 2–3

 Did your acquaintances make dire predictions when you told them of your plans? Were predictions for you, as for Mary Kingsley, like a gauntlet thrown down which you then felt bound to take up?

 Who were your informants — college teachers, previous travelers, books, movies? Were they seeing the country and culture for itself, or, like the missionaries to whom Kingsley talked and whose stories she read, only reporting how they thought the country and culture should be according to their own standards and ideals? What ideas and impressions fed to you before departure have you been challenged to shed? Have any puzzling situations been made clear?

Sana Hasan

I sat outside by the entrance, where the truck was expected to pull up, waiting for the other volunteers to finish their breakfast.

The first to arrive was a slender, dark girl wearing a long lilac skirt, a flowery scarf, golden bangles, and hoop earrings. She could have been an Egyptian peasant dressed up for the Mulid (the celebration of the Prophet's birthday), but she turned out to be from Tashkent. Next came an English redhead in a sequin-studded blouse with a low-cut, frilly neckline. She was full of coquettish affectations, and she had a strong cockney accent. Having tried her luck with the girl from Tashkent to no avail (the latter spoke no English), she began to talk to me. Fortunately, however, a young man from Brazil made his appearance, and I was abandoned in favor of this more attractive target. Soon our working team of twenty-four people was complete, and we waited for the pickup truck.

We drove across a terrain bordered by mauve mountain slopes. Their barrenness contrasted with the richness of the fields. Our truck cut a swath through the dark, moist layers of earth, which crumbled on contact with the wheels like the frosting of a chocolate cake. A strong odor of freshly tilled sod filled the air. No wonder the pioneers fell in love with this land; no wonder the Palestinians refused to leave it.

The truck dropped us off at the edge of the potato plots; behind them towered a whole field of sunflowers, bowing under the weight of their crowns. After a while, our overseers arrived — all of them strongly built men, and all of them bare-chested. Nowhere was the difference between the generation of Eastern European pioneers and their offspring more apparent than on the kibbutz. The young people, a whole head taller than their parents, looked like another species.

How we volunteers admired those powerful sunburned torsos that glistened like liquid gold! But these handsome, proud sons of Israel had nothing but disdain for us. To them, we were only a pack of spoiled visitors who regarded their work on the kibbutz as an exotic way to spend a summer vacation before returning once more to their pampered, bourgeois lives.

Enemy in the Promised Land, 92–93

Sana Hasan is one of many who have come to Israel to serve on a kibbutz. And the kibbutzim are among the thousands of places around the world where the foreign volunteer and the local resident serve side by side. It is not always an easy relationship.

 What have you experienced? What accounts for the attitudes of the agency staff? If you have met with hostility or indifference, what have you done to change the relationship? Have you succeeded?

 If you have known only welcome, to whom do you attribute this good fortune? Your manners? Past volunteers? The generosity of the staff? The wisdom and management of the supervisor?

SAMUEL JOHNSON

The city of St. Andrews, when it had lost its archiepiscopal pre-eminence, gradually decayed; one of its streets is now lost; and in those that remain there is the silence and solitude of inactive indulgence and gloomy depopulation.

The university, within a few years, consisted of three colleges, but is now reduced to two; the college of St. Leonard being lately dissolved by the sale of its buildings and the appropriation of its revenues to the professors of the two others. The chapel of the alienated college is yet standing, a fabric not inelegant of external structure; but I was always, by some civil excuse, hindered from entering it. A decent attempt, as I was since told, has been made to convert it into a kind of green-house, by planting its area with shrubs. This new method of gardening is unsuccessful; the plants do not hitherto prosper. To what use it will next be put I have no pleasure in conjecturing. It is something that its present state is at least not ostentatiously displayed. Where there is yet shame there may in time be virtue.

The dissolution of St. Leonard's College was doubtless necessary; but of that necessity there is reason to complain. It is surely not without just reproach that a nation, of which the commerce is hourly extending, and the wealth increasing, denies any participation of its prosperity to its literary societies; and, while its merchants or its nobles are raising palaces, suffers its universities to moulder into dust.

Having now seen whatever this ancient city offered to our curiosity, we left it with good wishes, having reason to be highly pleased with the attention that was paid us. But whoever surveys the world must see many things that give him pain. The kindness of the professors did not contribute to abate the uneasy remembrance of a university declining, a college alienated and a church profaned and hastening to the ground.

A Journey to the Western Islands of Scotland, 8–11

Here we were met by a post-chaise that conveyed us to Glasgow...[where there is] prosperity of commerce...[but] the college has not had a sufficient share of the increasing magnificence of the place. The session was begun (for it commences on the 10th of October and continues to the 10th of June), but the students appeared not numerous, being, I suppose, not yet returned from their several homes. The division of the academical year into one session and one recess, seems to me better accommodated to the present state of life than variegation of time, by terms and vacations, derived from distant centuries, in which it was probably convenient, and still continued in English Universities. So many solid months as the Scotch scheme of education joins together, allow and encourage a plan for each part of the year; but with us, he that has settled himself to study in the college is soon tempted into the country, and he that has adjusted his life in the country is summoned back to his college.

Yet when I have allowed to the Universities of Scotland a more rational distribution of time, I have given them, so far as my inquiries have informed me, all that they can claim. The students for the most part, go thither boys and depart before they are men; they carry with them little fundamental knowledge, and therefore the superstructure cannot be lofty. The grammar schools are not generally well supplied; for the character of a schoolmaster, being there less honourable than in England, is seldom accepted by men who are capable to adorn it, and where the school has been deficient, the college can effect little.

Men bred in the Universities of Scotland cannot be expected to be often decorated with the splendours of ornamental erudition, but they obtain a mediocrity of knowledge, between learning and ignorance, not inadequate to the purposes of common life, which is, I believe, very widely diffused among them, and which, countenanced in general by a national combination so invidious that their friends cannot defend it, and actuated in particulars by a spirit of enterprise so vigorous that their enemies are constrained to praise it, enables them to find, or make their way to employment, riches, and distinction.

A Journey to the Western Islands of Scotland, 233–235

Johnson's first experience with education in Scotland was with the famous St. Andrew's University; the second was with the University of Glasgow, where his original judgment was confirmed. (Yet Glasgow was the University of Adam Smith, and later Lord Kelvin and a host of other luminaries.)

 Systems of education and forms of teaching vary from country to country. What have you discovered about the system of education in your host nation? What place does education hold in the values of the nation? Is there a difference between the rhetoric and the reality? How do you relate the form and quality of education to national achievement?

A major task before the student abroad is that of understanding the structures and pedagogy of education. Sometimes students fail to learn all they might in their new school because they are wedded to the way they were previously taught and judge any difference as inferior.

 What are the underlying assumptions of the system and form of education in your home country and in your host country? What is the role of the student and the teacher? By what measures are you judging the practices of the teachers in your host institution? Do you agree with the Partnership policy of using teachers indigenous to the culture rather than sending a U.S. professor to accompany and teach you? Why do you think we made that choice for our programs? What benefits and what limitations does this decision pose?

JANE ADDAMS

It was during this second journey to Europe that I attended a meeting of the London match girls who were on strike and who met daily under the leadership of well-known labor men of London. The low wages that were reported at the meetings, the phossy jaw which was described and occasionally exhibited, the appearance of the girls themselves I did not, curiously enough, in any wise connect with what was called the labor movement, nor did I understand the efforts of the London trades-unionists, concerning whom I held the vaguest notions. But of course this impression of human misery was added to the others which were already making me so wretched. I think that up to this time I was still filled with the sense which Wells describes in one of his young characters, that somewhere in Church or State are a body of authoritative people who will put things to rights as soon as they really know what is wrong. Such a young person persistently believes that behind all suffering, behind sin and want, must lie redeeming magnanimity. He may imagine the world to be tragic and terrible, but it never for an instant occurs to him that it may be contemptible or squalid or self-seeking. Apparently I looked upon the efforts of the trades-unionists as I did upon those of Frederic Harrison and the Positivists whom I heard the next Sunday in Newton Hall, as a manifestation of "loyalty to humanity" and an attempt to aid in its progress.

Twenty Years at Hull-House, 57–58

One challenge for any hero lies in understanding the nature, character, and motives of individuals or groups with whom she must work. Jane Addams admits missing the connection between the labor movement and the conditions experienced by the match girls.

 What connections have you made between what you see through your agency and political activities in your host country?

 What experience have you had in which you changed your mind about an organization or changed your way of dealing with a person? Did you become more trusting of the people or group or less so?

 Do you believe, as did Addams at one time, that people will generally "put things to rights as soon as they really know what is wrong" and that behind the apparent suffering lies "redeeming magnanimity?" What do you believe about the concept of progress?

ANTHONY WINKLER

I did not understand then how Americans think about race. Later, after I had lived there for a while and seen a white woman crowned Miss America who the press insisted was black, after I came to understand that on racial matters Americans are the world's most consummate casuists, it all became clearer to me. But that was only years later. When I had the confrontation with this manager I had been in America for only three months and my head was still in a whirl.

Americans see colour strictly as a consanguineous and physical quality: it is to them so much a matter of blood that a pint inherited from a great-great-great black ancestor is enough to classify anyone as black no matter how white he may look. Jamaicans, and West Indians as a whole, regard colour as inseparable from manners, behaviour, background, education, and culture — that whole constellation of traits the Englishman once labelled "breeding." This fundamental and deep-rooted difference between Americans and Jamaicans, and possibly all Caribbean peoples, may in part be responsible for the antagonism that some say exists between American blacks and blacks from the West Indies.

It is not difficult to understand how Jamaicans and West Indians came to think about race as they do. Simple mimicry of the English was to blame. When the Englishman was plundering the world during his colonialist binge, the standard he carried everywhere around with him was his precious English culture. Take the most uncouth English second son and plant him among black people on a distant shore, and overnight he became oppressively boorish and legalistic about his customs and manners. If he had dropped his "h's" like flies in London, he tacked them on again scrupulously while bawling for his slave in Jamaica. If he had never read a book in his life in Yorkshire, in Jamaica he acquired the airs of a pedant. Away

114

from home, he was suddenly obsessed with preserving and practising English ideals and virtues with an unslaked passion.

Part of this pose was a defence against being engulfed by the preponderant black races among whom he had been posted. George Orwell, who was himself part of the colonial shock troops sent to subdue India, wrote that the Englishman abroad lived in terror of losing face. Death by pillorying was preferable to public embarrassment before the hordes of savages among whom he was supposed to spread enlightenment. Keeping a stout English face, putting on a good front, became the primal duty of the colonial.

This effort made the colonial Englishman a figure so clotted with distinctive mannerisms, ceremonies, and pretensions as to be ludicrously theatrical. The slaves witnessed this white man daily enacting his bizarre theatre of what it was like to be English and thought to themselves: so that's what it means to be white. As the more venturesome among them rose to positions of favouritism and prominence, they aped their masters with a vengeance; and colour became equated with a certain cast of mind and mannerisms of behaviour. The equation has persisted to this day in Jamaica.

There was no explaining all this to Cathy. In any event, explanations alone cannot condition you to live among the peculiar cultural worldview of a people. Only experience can truly teach about culture, and, now that she was living among my people, she would have to learn to grapple with their ways of thinking and behaving. It was plainly a difficult and painful experience for her, and in her struggle she reminded me of my paternal grandmother, who lives in my memory as the classic example of a maladjusted white foreigner.

Going Home to Teach, 80–81

One of the most difficult challenges is understanding the meaning of race and class in a culture other than one's own.

 When was the difference between your view and that of the host culture made evident to you? Perhaps you will want to recount a telling incident.

 How have you come to understand the difference? What have you learned in your study of the history of your host nation about how attitudes regarding class and race came to be formed? In your host culture, is there a rhetoric about these issues that is commonly voiced? What have you observed in practice? Is it consistent or inconsistent with the rhetoric and in what ways?

 Do you agree with Anthony Winkler that there are some difficult issues such as race and class which do not yield to explanation but can only be experienced?

OCTAVIO PAZ

Music was another initiation, more extensive and more noble; I confess that in that art, as in so many other things, I continue to be a novice. I say this with a certain sadness, considering that it has been my constant companion for years. I listened to it in concert on memorable nights in the gardens of Delhi, mingled with the rustle of the wind in the leaves; other times I heard it slipping into my room like a sinuous river, sometimes dark and sometimes sparkling. Ragas are soliloquies and meditations, passionate melodies that draw circles and triangles in a mental space, a geometry of sounds that can turn a room into a fountain, a spring, a pool. What I learned from music — besides the pleasure of walking through those galleries of echoes and gardens of transparent trees, where sounds think and thoughts dance — was something that I also found in Indian poetry and thought: the tension between wholeness and emptiness, the continual coming and going between the two.

Sculpture was my first revelation and remains the most enduring. Not only the works from the high periods, such as those on Elephanta, but also the small wonders that are the popular works, made of clay, metal, or wood, sonorous as birds, fantastic forms born from the hands of anonymous craftsmen. Indian sculpture is naturalistic, like that of Greece or Rome, and is the aesthetic opposite of the sculpture of ancient Mexico, that lover of terrible abstractions. But in their folk arts the Indian and Mexican sensibilities converge: fantasy, humor, bright colors, bizarre shapes. The world of an ordinary sacredness and of a daily poetry. The love of objects that function as talismans, utensils, or toys is central to the Indian sensibility. Essential, too, is an affinity for nomenclatures, numbers, categories, and lists, whether of shapes, tastes or sensations, philosophical ideas, or grammatical figures. Logic, grammar, aesthetics, and erotics are alike in this predilection for catalogs and classifications.

The treatises on the erotic are dictionaries of positions, caresses, and sensations.

At the same time, there is a passion for unity. It is not by chance that India discovered the zero; nor that it was seen simultaneously as a mathematical concept and a metaphysical reality. For Shankara, one is the limit of the thinkable; for Nagarjuna, emptiness is. Between the one and the zero—incessant combat and instantaneous embrace—the history of Indian thought unfolds. The great questions about the reality of the world—What is it? How is it?—also encompass the question of origin: What was there at the beginning? Was there a beginning? In one of the most beautiful hymns of the Rig Veda, sometimes called the "Hymn of Creation," the poet tries to imagine how it was at the beginning and asks:

> Then even nothingness was not, nor existence.
>> There was no air then, nor the heavens beyond it.
> What covered it? Where was it? In whose keeping?
>> Was there then cosmic water, in depths unfathomed?
>
> Then there was neither death nor immortality,
>> nor was there then the torch of night and day.
> The One breathed mindlessly and self-sustaining.
>> There was that One then, and there was no other.[10]

In Light of India, 138–139

An essential tool for understanding a culture is its art, philosophy, and intellectual achievements.

 What have you learned in class, on field trips, or through your own exploring that has helped you understand the people with whom you live and work? (We hope you could here form a long list!) Pick one or two ideas or works of art on which to focus. What characteristics do these ideas or works illustrate or reveal about your host culture?

LANGSTON HUGHES

Six months anywhere is enough to begin to complicate life. By that time, if you stay in one place, you are bound to know people too well for things to be any longer simple. Well, that winter one of my pupils fell in love with me.

The Big Sea, 67

Langston Hughes declares that it takes time for newcomers to become part of the culture and for relationships to develop — and that when this happens it complicates life.

 Have you seen your relationship with individuals or your understanding of the culture become more complicated as your stay lengthens? How long do you think it takes to begin to understand and be part of the complexities?

 Have you, in any sense of the phrase, fallen in love? Has anyone fallen in love with you? Is the love realistic or a romantic dream?

SAMUEL JOHNSON

At last we came to Icolmkill, but found no convenience for landing. Our boat could not be forced very near the dry ground, and our Highlanders carried us over the water.

We were now treading that illustrious island, which was once the luminary of the Caledonian regions, whence savage clans and roving barbarians derived the benefits of knowledge and the blessings of religion. To abstract the mind from all local emotion would be impossible if it were endeavoured, and would be foolish if it were possible. Whatever withdraws us from the power of our senses; whatever makes the past, the distant, or the future predominate over the present, advances us in the dignity of thinking beings. Far from me and from my friends be such frigid philosophy as may conduct us indifferent and unmoved over any ground which has been dignified by wisdom, bravery, or virtue.

A Journey to the Western Islands of Scotland, 217

Samuel Johnson was writing of the most famous and, to the Scots, the most sacred of Islands—Iona—where Columba, a follower of St. Patrick, first established Christianity in Scotland and where generations of medieval kings are buried.

 What does Johnson mean when he says that "abstracting the mind from local emotion" is "impossible" and would be "foolish?" Have you visited places which are special to the local inhabitants? How has such a visit helped you to understand the values and beliefs of the people?

 Has a "frigid philosophy" stood in the way of your full appreciation of those places and of the history and beliefs they symbolize?

Langston Hughes

When I got word that my father was dead, the word came at second-hand. What happened was that a wire in Spanish had come for me to Carmel. The Filipino houseboy had relayed it to a friend of mine, who attempted to translate it, and who, in turn, advised me by wire in English to Reno that my father had died and the estate awaited my claim. I had at that moment less than a hundred dollars, not nearly enough for a trip to Mexico City. The only other relative my father had to whom he wrote was a sister in Indianapolis. I phoned her and asked what she thought I should do. My aunt — Aunt Sallie — advised me to go to Mexico right away and see about the property. Since she could not speak Spanish, but might perhaps be an heir — indeed felt sure that she was — she would lend me the money for the trip.

Aunt Sallie wired me three hundred dollars. The next day I took my first plane flight — from Reno over the mountains to San Francisco. There I picked up the original wire from Mexico. In Spanish what it really said was not that the estate awaited my arrival to receive it, but that the reading of the will awaited my coming. Since my father and I never liked each other, I doubted he had left me anything. But, since I loved Mexico, I didn't mind going there again. Twenty-four hours outside of Mexico City, on the train, I suddenly remembered how much Mexicans go in for mourning. I had not even a dark suit nor a black tie to wear, let alone a mourning band on my arm. And I was my father's only son!

My father had lived in Mexico for thirty years. During that long period his best friends had been three very devout Catholic ladies, unmarried sisters, one of whom had looked after his real estate, and all of whom had cared for him during his illness. These gentle women had cared for me as a child, and I loved them. Each time that I had been to Mexico and had seen them, they had always been deep in mourning for somebody, all in

121

black from head to toe — since Mexican women of the old school love to mourn for even very distant relatives. I knew these elderly sisters would expect me to be wearing black for my father. Since I was certain they would meet me at the station, my stomach began to turn over with anxiety. How could I avoid startling their sense of propriety when I got off the train in California sport clothes — with nothing black at all?

Fortunately, the train was scheduled to stop an hour at Guadalajara. I thought that there I could find a shop near the station and at least buy a black tie and a crepe band for my arm. But when we got to Guadalajara, it was a Saint's Day of some kind, so all the shops were closed. In desperation out of my luggage I took a dark blue tie with canary polka dots and, with the ink from my fountain pen, attempted to color the yellow dots black, so that I would at least be wearing a dark tie upon my arrival at the capital in the morning. Over my berth I hung the tie up to dry when I retired. The next day just before arriving in Mexico City, when I went to put the tie on, to my consternation the chemicals in the ink had only changed the yellow polka dots to a bright green! When the three Patiño sisters met me at the station, all in black themselves and weeping, I had no semblance of mourning on. But when I got to their house, one of them quickly made for me a black arm band as they told me the circumstances of my father's death.

The Big Sea, 287–289

Understanding a culture and its most cherished customs is a primary challenge for the hero abroad. All travelers have the need at one time or another to try to cover a cultural gaffe.

 What such experience have you had? How did you try to "make it right" and what was the result?

EMILY BRONSON CONGER

The next morning we took our guide and three natives to each foreigner to assist in getting us up the Nikko mountain. It took from 7 o'clock in the morning until 2 in the afternoon to reach the summit. Every mountain peak was covered with red, white, and pink azaleas. Our pathway was over a carpet of the petals of these exquisite blooms. We used every glowing adjective that we could command at every turn of these delightful hills.

There is a great waterfall in the hills, some two hundred fifty feet high.

On returning we were often obliged to alight and walk over fallen boulders, this being the first trip after the winter snows. At one place, being "overtoppled" by the weight of my clothes and the cramped position that I had been in, I lost my balance and fell down, it seemed to me to be about a mile and a half. In a moment there were at least fifty pairs of hands to assist me up the mountain side. A dislocated wrist, a battered nose, and a blackened eye was the inventory of damages. Such a chattering as those natives did set up, while I, with a bit of medical skill, which I am modestly proud of, attended to my needs. The day had been so full of delights that I did not mind being battered and bruised, nor did I lose appetite for the very fine dinner we had at the Nikko Hotel, so daintily served in the most attractive fashion by the little Japanese maidens in their dainty costumes. In the evening the hotel became a lively bazaar.

An Ohio Woman in the Philippines, 23–24

Some heroes minimize or even deny their difficulties, a response which can limit the opportunity for learning and can even endanger them or others. Other heroes, out of need for comfort, drama or attention, exaggerate the difficulties. Could Emily Conger really have enjoyed her evening of dinner and the bazaar had she had so severe an injury as she reports in her narrative?

Learning to see experiences in a balanced way and to record honestly and accurately is a major task for the hero who will one day be recognized as a leader.

 Have you denied or inflated any difficulty you have faced? Are you able to identify why you did or were tempted to do so? What was the result?

PAUL COWAN

In nearly every Peace Corps group there is one person whose apparent success with host-country nationals becomes legendary, a fantasy for his peers that sometimes carries them through their own relative failures. He is the Supervolunteer: the Peace Corps' Kit Carson, uniquely equipped to find his way through the alien territory.

The Supervolunteer in Guayaquil was the only member of his group who expressly refrained from adopting the macho attitudes that most community developers believed were essential in Latin America. A devout Catholic, he rarely got drunk and refused to go out whoring. We met him the night before he was supposed to return to the States, and he gave me the same impression of slightly grubby self-confident toughness that I found among city-born Israelis who had lived on a kibbutz for several years and convinced themselves that they really could survive under physically taxing circumstances.

He spoke gently, and very honestly, about his relations with the Ecuadorians in his barrio. It was clear that be had forced himself to accept the fact that they would never change as rapidly as he thought they could, forced himself to accept their traditions and customs although he did not particularly enjoy them. But he was a simpler person than Margot and therefore able to accept relationships that left her feeling thoroughly dissatisfied; and he was much kinder than the volunteer who wanted to shoot surrogate Ecuadorians in Vietnam. He was as patient as a man can be, and I'm sure that no other quality was so important to his success.

The community where he lived was even farther from the center of town than Margot's, about forty-five minutes by bus, and when its people got sick they were often unable to journey all the way to the city's hospitals. Anyway, most of them were too poor to pay for medical treatment. So the Supervolunteer encouraged them to build a health center where they would be examined gratis by doctors who would commute to the barrios several times a week.

The Supervolunteer had organized the labor in a way that in theory made great sense. The people, directed by their comité would build the structure for the health center; the Peace Corps would devise a regular schedule the doctors could follow; AID would furnish the roof.

But it turned out that the Supervolunteer had to hold the entire project together by the force of his own personality. The comité was so torn by quarrels and jealousies that, without his presence, his constant manipulation, it would have dissolved long ago. The Ecuadorians distrusted each other so much, he said, that they had finally appointed him to serve as the comité's treasurer because he was the only person whom the community felt it could trust with the funds.

He had even more trouble sustaining the doctors' commitment to the project than his neighbors'. Each afternoon he would make the long bus ride into town, hire a taxi, stop at their offices, and shepherd them out to the barrio in time for their appointments. The doctors never traveled out there alone, and they were very reluctant to use the bus.

Finally, AID had not yet delivered the roof it promised. The Supervolunteer felt that the Peace Corps would have to keep badgering her sister organization until the day when its officials felt so guilty that they would organize a big public ceremony, invite the press, and dedicate the health center in the name of the Alliance for Progress and Ecuadorian-American friendship. But AID was a big bureaucracy, and guilt, even self-interested guilt, was not an emotion many of its employees developed very quickly.

The Supervolunteer was an artist: he had done a masterful job of harmonizing many divergent interests. But community development was supposed to be an applied science, a technique that any reasonably intelligent person could learn in two months. Could Sid Raschi, the less talented, less dedicated volunteer who would move into his community, sustain the enthusiasm that Supervolunteer had created? It sounded, rather, as if the flimsy structure of human relationships he had been propping up would collapse before the health center was completed.

And if successful community-development projects required the sustained presence of Super-volunteers then how could the rest of us — or the Ecuadorians themselves — hope to accomplish even the tasks that had sounded relatively simple in training, let alone the special jobs that we had been assigned to do?

The Making of an Un-American, 180–182

The greatest challenge for anyone in community service is that of building a project that will become self-sustaining. There is a great temptation to become the charismatic leader enjoying all the power and admiration that term implies.

 What do you know about the history of the organization in which you are serving? Does its success now depend on a charismatic leader? What do you believe is the long-term future of the agency and its work? Is it self-sustaining, and if not, what might be changed to make it so?

 Have you seen other service projects that are failing for lack of community commitment?

 Have you seen or even yourself been the "Supervolunteer" whom Cowan describes? What have you done or might you do to ensure that your effort goes on even after you have returned home?

SANA HASAN

As I was hurrying away from the mobbed beach, I noticed a large crowd in front of a theater. I did not know if the film was any good, but I knew it was a chance for a few quiet moments in a cool, air-conditioned place. When I got closer I saw they were lining up to see *The Towering Inferno*. I bought a ticket and walked in. Since no usher was in sight, I picked out a seat at random. No sooner had the feature begun than Russian curses rent the air, followed by a crash of broken glass and furious screams. I jumped out of my seat, ready to rush to the door, but the woman next to me caught my sleeve, forcing me to sit down. "Don't worry," she said in English. "I see you are a foreigner. It's nothing. This happens all the time in Israel. Someone must have sat in someone else's seat, and there's a fight. That's all."…

I soon realized, in Israel it was a time-honored custom to talk uninterruptedly through movies. In this case, since most of the audience did not understand English, it hardly paid to listen anyway. My own command of English yielded me no advantage, for the hubbub totally drowned out the voices of the actors. Fortunately, someone had had the foresight to insert French subtitles in addition to the Hebrew ones. To the murmur of voices was added the continuous crackling of sunflower seeds, which Israelis seemed to consume in enormous quantities, and the wailing of a baby.

The rest of the movie unfolded uneventfully to the accompaniment of the audience's running commentary. As the movie fire spread in a newly built skyscraper during its inauguration ceremony, the audience shouted advice to the hero, Steve McQueen, who was in charge of the rescue operation. "*Lo, lo mikan, idiot!*" ("No, not here, idiot!"), someone would call out to him as he tried to elude the flames. Catcalls and hisses would follow. "*Ta'azov oto, hu mistader tov me'od*" ("Get off his back, he's doing fine"), another viewer would respond. *"Eze chor batacbat! Tishbor et hachalon!"* ("What an asshole! Smash the window!"), a third person would yell. The heckling gave way to smacks and sharp whistles whenever a romantic love scene alternated with the action. I giggled as I remembered how my father had refused to set foot in movie theaters ever since the revolution had allowed the populace to invade the balconies, bringing their sunflower seeds and lewd jokes with them. And I thought of how Theodor Herzl, the founder of the Jewish state, would turn in his grave if only he could see how his dream of building a Viennese polity in the Middle East had fared. Had he not rallied the Jews to form "a wall of defense for Europe in Asia, an outpost of civilization against barbarism"?

It occurred to me then that perhaps Israel's desire to perceive herself as part of Europe was a way of gaining the acceptance historically denied to the Jews. Building a second Vienna in Israel would certainly prove to the West, which had humiliated and rejected them, that the Jews were every bit as civilized as any people in Europe.

I, too, had expected that Tel Aviv would be like Vienna, but there in the dark theater, tired, sunburned, exhilarated, I realized that I felt disturbingly at home in this city, because, with its shabby four-story houses, its balconies, its teeming beaches, and its people's endearing vulgarity, it could have been Alexandria.

Enemy in the Promised Land, 44–45

Giving up the predeparture image of the new land and its people is a challenge for all sojourners. It often comes from an intense experience such as the one Sana Hasan had in the movie theater.

 What images have been hard for you to relinquish? What made you finally see in a new or more complete light?

Another important challenge is also contained in this passage — that of recognizing similarities. In traveling abroad, we usually expect and look for differences. Finding those things held in common between the home and host cultures may be the more difficult task, especially if the similarities flatter neither.

 What similarities have you recognized?

KATHLEEN NORRIS

On a crowded planet, this is a place inhabited by few, and by the circumstance of inheritance, I am one of them. Nearly twenty years ago I returned to the holy ground of my childhood summers; I moved from New York City to the house my mother had grown up in, in an isolated town on the border between North and South Dakota.

More than any other place I lived as a child or young adult — Virginia, Illinois, Hawaii, Vermont, New York — this is my spiritual geography, the place where I've wrestled my story out of the circumstances of landscape and inheritance. The word "geography" derives from the Greek words for earth and writing, and writing about Dakota has been my means of understanding that inheritance and reclaiming what is holy in it. Of course Dakota has always been such a matrix for its Native American inhabitants. But their tradition is not mine, and in returning to the Great Plains, where two generations of my family lived before me, I had to build on my own traditions, those of the Christian West.

Dakota: A Spiritual Geography, 2–3

 Is this program of service-learning an "inheritance journey" for you in any way? Does your family have roots, however distant, in the country you have chosen? As a result of your time in the new land, have your ideas and feelings changed about your "inheritance?" Do you feel more, or less, "at one" with your heritage?

 Is there a connection through your previous academic study to either the location you have chosen or to your service? Have you "a spiritual affinity?"

 Kathleen Norris saw her task as that of reclaiming the holy out of her inheritance. What do you see as your task?

STAGE VI

BATTLING
THE BEASTS

W here would the hero be without the dragon or giant to slay? All heroes, as they venture forth to accomplish the given tasks, face perils to themselves and to the communities through which they pass.

As the hero begins the journey, she looks back at the receding vision of the safe and familiar and looks forward to a path the character and direction of which she cannot yet know. This is the point in the journey in which her old synthesis of meaning, values, beliefs, and relationships is breaking down, a necessary step if a new one is to emerge. In myth, this period is often portrayed as a sailor afloat on an open sea, with exciting, new lands to discover but also carrying the impression of having been cut adrift.

Alone and without already tested aids, she comes upon labyrinthine caves of fire-breathing dragons, raging seas of leviathans, deep jungles filled with hungry lions and venomous snakes, parched deserts beckoning with their deceptive mirages and evil cities of clever tempters. These are the metaphors, repeated in story after story, culture after culture, for the battles we must fight along the way to transformation.

Those who study the phenomenon of culture shock tell us that for those planning a journey of three to four months, this stage is concentrated around five weeks into the journey. It is a time when the beast of exhaustion from the physical, intellectual, and emotional effort of relating to a strange culture takes its toll. The earlier exhilaration gives way to feelings of loneliness, depression, exaggerated fears, disappointment, annoyance, and inadequacy, leaving the unreflective hero blaming others and excusing himself. The hero may seek a way out. Some actually return home, but most, in story and real life, beat only a temporary retreat to marshal their strength and prepare for a new battle.

This stage is also the point at which the brave hero begins to be recognized as worthy of the leadership position he will one day assume. Here he demonstrates that he is able to put aside his own feelings, fears, and needs in order to do the job that must be done for himself and for others. No longer expecting others to save him, he picks up the sword and steps forward, confident of his ability to overcome his fear, anger, disappointment, weakness, frustration, or ignorance. Psychologists say that in the journey to adulthood this stage marks the passage from a narcissistic focus, characteristic of adolescents, to maturity, in which, as adults, we are able to control our feelings and by an act of will work selflessly for the good of others.

Naming the beast—recognizing it for what it is—is the first step toward slaying it. Reflecting upon and writing about the beasts they battled on their journeys, our diarists were able to identify their own points of weakness and vulnerability, and thus find the magic sword for conquering the threats to their proceeding on the journey. They grew stronger from the battles. So will you.

Anthony Winkler

I have always been a bad first-time lecturer. My heart trips and hammers, my throat becomes dry, I stand before the class struggling inwardly against hysteria and paralysis. The first word must be said and said quickly to overcome this fear, and usually when I bound into a classroom on the initial meeting I come bearing buoyant platitude or hearty greeting just so I can quickly break the ice. This first time in a Jamaican classroom was no different. If anything, it was worse because I desperately wanted to make a good impression on my students.

There was the long walk down the paved walkway past the royal palms and the towering flame heart trees, and then the unnerving climb up the soiled concrete steps and into the maw of the classroom where the students were already assembled and waiting. I stepped inside and they all jumped to attention like soldiers on parade. I stopped dead in the doorway, my mind in a whirl, until I remembered that this standing at attention when the teacher enters the classroom was a courtesy drilled into all Jamaican students from infancy and one that I myself used to practice. So here was my chance to break the ice: do away with this obsolete courtesy left over by the excessively ceremonious Englishman.

I placed my books on the desk and waved the students to be seated.

"From now on," I began, hoping that my voice did not sound as croaky to them as it did to me, "don't stand up when I come into the classroom. I'm not used to that and it makes me uncomfortable. Just stay in your seats while I call the roll."

A stony silence greeted this announcement. I fumbled for the roll book and began calling off the names on the roster. With the first name, a student leapt to her feet and said, "Here, sah!"

"You don't have to stand up when I call your names," I said. "Just say, 'here'."

After I had read the roll and looked at every face and tried my best to attach a name to it, I stood up and gave an introductory speech. I told them my name, emphasized that I was a returning Jamaican, and said the usual nervous platitudes about hoping to get to know everyone and to have a good and fruitful year with the class. The students sat ominously silent. No one moved. Hardly anyone looked in my direction. Everyone seemed engrossed in studying their desk tops or observing unseen creatures on the concrete floor.

"Are there any questions?" I asked at the end of my speech.

Please ask a question, I whispered inwardly. Please ask anything just to help me over this hump.

No one said a word. No one stirred. No one looked at me. A doomsday silence swelled in the room. I glanced at the class. It consisted of some twenty-nine brown and black women and one effeminate black man who sat in the very back row, wore a jacket and tie, and was identified on the roll book as the Reverend Hamilton. I singled him out.

"Mr. Hamilton," I said over the rows and rows of expressionless faces, "I see that you're a minister. What denomination?"

"Church of the Holy Ghost, sah," he replied timidly in a falsetto voice.

A stout woman in the front row swivelled in her seat with effort and glared at him.

"No one is to talk, Hamilton!" she snapped.

"Sorry," he whispered, looking downcast.

"Why can't he talk?" I asked innocently. "He can talk if I ask him a question, can't he?"

The stout woman stared fixedly at the floor.

"What's your name?" I asked, the panic rising to flood spate. Something was amiss. They hated me so intensely at first sight that they had entered into a conspiracy never to breathe a word in my presence.

She did not answer.

"Why is no one to talk?"

Nothing. Not a sigh, not a whisper. Some where in the classroom a belly bubbled hungrily and in the deafening silence it sounded like a draining sink.

I walked from one end of the room to the other — keep moving, always keep moving in times of tension — looking them over with what I hoped was appropriate mystification and good will. Nothing. The most hideous display of deadpan.

"All right, then," I said firmly. "If we can't talk, at least we can write. This is an English class and we are going to be doing a lot of writing in it. We will write at least one composition a week. So take out your books and write a composition on your home town or village. I won't be marking it, I just want to get an idea of what kind of work you can do."

Not a single solitary soul moved. Not a finger lifted a pencil, not a hand touched an exercise book. They sat before me row after row of mummified, expressionless faces. I had made such a bad impression on them that right before my eyes they had been collectively struck dead. How would I explain that students entrusted to my care by the Jamaican government had all dropped dead the moment I began lecturing? My years of teaching American pothead students in California told me that there was only one graceful and intelligent thing to do: get the devil out of there before the class started decomposing.

"Well, in that case," I said in my huffiest tone, "you can carry on without a teacher."

I walked sternly and slowly out of the room like a postman bravely and desperately turning his back on a bad dog and went home.

It was a long and fretful weekend. My class had met on a Friday afternoon and I had two days to ponder what I would do on Monday, whether to throw myself at the mercy of the vice principal and confess that I had given my students a case of terminal catatonia, or to charge once more into the classroom and do my best to shake them out of their collective stupor.

"I can't believe this is happening to me," I told Cathy over and over again. "I just can't believe it! You should have seen them. They sat there and didn't say a word. Not a word!"

"There must be an explanation," she assured me. "Did you say something to upset them?"

"I told them my name."

"Don't be silly."

"I told them I was looking forward to spending the academic year with them. Maybe that was it? Maybe they found the idea so unbearable that they all passed out on the spot?"

"Did you give them homework?"

"Homework? I couldn't even get them to do classwork, much less homework! I asked them to write an essay just so I could see a sample of their work, and they didn't move. They just sat there!"

"There has to be an explanation."

"There is! They hate me! They can't stand the sight of me! That's the explanation!"

"They don't know you. How can they hate you?"

"God, I can't believe this is happening to me! On my first class meeting, too!"

Friday night passed like a funeral cortege. Cathy tried to cheer me up, but I was inconsolable. Saturday we went to the beach, but all I could think of was thirty glum faces staring impassively at me while I vainly tried to coax signs of life out of them. On Sunday I paced and brooded and went for a walk in the pastures during a drizzle and racked my brain for any hint of what I might have said or done to alienate the class and turn them all against me. Nothing occurred to me. Not a clue, not a glimmer, nothing at all.

That night as we sat with the Smiths having a drink in their drawing room and watching the sun set, all I could think about was that tomorrow I would once again have to brave that sea of hardened faces.

"How many students do you have in your class?" Cathy asked Derrick, trying to make conversation. He laughed.

"I'm not sure," he said. "They wouldn't answer the roll."

I nearly jumped out of my chair.

"Really?" I gasped.

"Yes. They're on strike. Cheeky! Sat there and wouldn't say a word. Wouldn't even answer when I called their names. Just sat there."

"They did!"

He seemed puzzled by the elation in my voice.

"They did the same to me, too," said Heather. "I got so mad I wanted to reach out and box one of their faces."

"They're on strike!" I gushed over and over to Cathy as we walked back to our house in the darkness. "The whole school is on strike! Isn't it wonderful?"

"I'm so happy for you, sweetheart," she murmured.

Going Home to Teach, 52–56

By his own admission, Anthony Winkler was so insecure about his ability to teach that he was sure that the situation he describes was due to his own personal inadequacy, when in fact it had nothing to do with him personally.

 Have you battled the beast of insecurity only to find that the cause of your failure lay elsewhere? How long did it take you to discover the real truth and how did your understanding come about?

The reverse situation may also be true. We sometimes give ourselves credit for something done well when in fact the credit belongs to others. Or we blame our failure on some other person or situation, thereby exonerating ourselves. Interpreting accurately is not an easy task, especially in another culture.

 Have you any examples to cite in which you struggled to assign responsibility to the correct source?

PAUL COWAN

Most of the trainees were very frightened. For many of them the Peace Corps was the first real test of a safe lifetime: strange people would be their superiors, an alien culture their home. Throughout training they waged a primal fight, against the tide of experience, to cling to the familiar world they understood.

They used nasty jokes, outright insults, to weld themselves together as a group and banish the unknown. As a result, the insensitivity many of them had absorbed from their families, friends, teachers, which they might have been able to control while they were still safe in Nixonia, began to seem like brutality when it was mixed in with their new fantasies and their new fears. In many cases, as the trainees passed through the looking glass of culture their ugliest features became the most prominent. Sometimes their behavior was silly, sometimes it was cruel. Always, their actions were rooted in their persistent, deepening desire to diminish the importance of anything unusual so that they could reassert their own superiority, or their manhood at least.

The Making of an Un-American, 125

Paul Cowan describes a situation in which volunteers tossed off crude jokes and made angry judgments about the very people they were to serve. He believes this behavior was motivated by a desire to assert their own superiority.

 Is it possible that there were other motivations for this behavior?

 A dragon with which the hero must do battle is that of seeing the fault of others without recognizing his own. Does Cowan realize his own need "to assert superiority" as he criticizes his colleagues? Have you any examples from your own experience?

 Have you observed the behavior of tourists or others new to a community, such as talking too loudly, showing excessive courtesy, acting inappropriately familiar, swaggering, or bragging about their home culture, that you suspect covers fears of not belonging? Would there have been a better way to conquer the beast of insecurity? How do you react to and handle these feelings in yourself?

Mary Kingsley

Now and again a man or woman [from the African bush] will come voluntarily and take service in Clarence, submit to clothes, and rapidly pick up the ways of a house or store. And just when their owner thinks he owns a treasure, and begins to boast that he has got an exception to all Bubidom, or else that he knows how to manage them better than other men, then a hole in that man's domestic arrangements suddenly appears. The Bubi has gone, without giving a moment's warning, and without stealing his master's property, but just softly and silently vanished away. And if hunted up the treasure will be found in his or her particular village — clothesless, comfortable, utterly unconcerned, and unaware that he or she has lost anything by leaving Clarence and civilisation. It is this conduct that gains for the Bubi the reputation of being a bigger idiot than he really is.

Travels in West Africa, 62

One of the frustrations that may beset the volunteer is finding that the opportunity she offers and believes is so very important is in fact given a low priority by those to whom the opportunity is offered. The child or adult fails to come to class regularly, the medical prescription is never filled, the micro-business loan is used for purposes other than developing the business — these leave the teacher, doctor, or economic developer profoundly disappointed.

 Have you experienced such frustrations? What conditions of people's lives or cultural values prevent their taking full advantage of the service you and your agency offer? How does this kind of experience change your notion of service? Are you imposing your sense of progress on a people for whom this is an alien notion of human life?

 Are you battling frustration in not fully accomplishing your goals for service? What weapons are you employing in the battle?

KATHLEEN NORRIS

Like ethnic peoples all over the world, Dakotans are in danger of becoming victims of their own mythology. As our towns are failing and our lives here become less viable, many Dakotans cling stubbornly to a myth of independence and local control that makes it difficult for us to come together and work for the things that might benefit us all. We've been slow to recognize that our traditional divisiveness (country versus town, small town versus city) makes us weak, not strong. As one North Dakota official recently put it, "We talk about a global society ... for crying out loud, we have to open our eyes and become a state society first."

Dakota: A Spiritual Geography, 32–33

Mythologies are meant to elevate and reveal truth, but sometimes they serve to distort.

 Are there mythologies getting in the way of the mission of your service agency? How do you understand the conflict of values and beliefs? Is one right and the other wrong?

 How have you interpreted your own culture to your hosts? Is the mythology you have shared with them an accurate reading of your own culture? What have you withheld? Why?

 What delusions do you recognize in yourself, your host culture, and your home culture that need to be dispelled?

143

EMILY BRONSON CONGER

I would take pail, scrubbing brush and lye, and fall to;... I would give an Akron rub myself to my own clothes.... These attacks of energy depended somewhat on the temperature, somewhat on exhausted patience, somewhat on home-sickness....

I smile now, not gaily, at the picture of myself over a washtub ... rubbing briskly while the tears of homesickness rolled down in uncontrollable floods, but singing, nevertheless, with might and main:

> "Am I a soldier of the Cross,
>   A follower of the Lamb?
> And shall I fear to own His cause,
>   Or blush to speak His name?
>
> "Must I be carried to the skies
>   On flowery beds of ease,
> While others fought to win the prize,
>   And sailed through bloody seas?"

Singing as triumphantly as possible to the last verse and word of that ringing hymn. My door and windows were set thick with wondering faces and staring eyes, a Señora washing. These Americans were past understanding!

An Ohio Woman in the Philippines, 158–159

When faced with the beasts of "exhausted patience" and "home-sickness," Emily Conger fell back on two deeply ingrained Ohio habits — house cleaning and hymn singing. They served her well.

 What habits do you seize as weapons when you confront loneliness, anxiety, or other beasts you meet along the way?

 Have any of these "weapons" alarmed, amused, or angered your hosts?

LANGSTON HUGHES

Hurry up! My father had tremendous energy. He always walked fast and rode hard. He was small and tough, like a jockey. He got up at five in the morning and worked at his accounts or his mail or his law books until time to go to the office. Then until ten or eleven o'clock at night he would be busy at various tasks, stopping only to eat. Then, on the days he made the long trek to the ranch, he rose at three-thirty or four, in order to get out there early and see what his workers were doing. Every one else worked too slowly for him, so it was always, "Hurry up!"

As the weeks went by, I could think of less and less to say to my father. His whole way of living was so different from mine, his attitude toward life and people so amazing, that I fell silent and couldn't open my mouth when he was in the house. Not even when he barked: "Hurry up!"

I hadn't heard from my mother, even by July. I knew she was angry with me because I had gone to Mexico. I understood then, though, why she had been unable to live with my father, and I didn't blame her. But why had she married him in the first place, I wondered. And why had they had me? Now, at seventeen, I began to be very sorry for myself, in a strange land in a mountain town, where there wasn't a person who spoke English. It was very cold at night and quiet, and I had no money to get away, and I was lonesome. I began to wish I had never been born—not under such circumstances.

I took long rides on a black horse named Tito to little villages of adobe huts, nestled in green fields of corn and alfalfa, little villages, each with a big church with a beautiful tower built a hundred years ago, a white Spanish tower with great bells swinging in the turret.

I began to learn to read Spanish. I struggled with bookkeeping. I took one of the old pistols from my father's desk and fired away in the afternoon at a target Maximiliano had put up in the corral. But most of the time I was depressed and unhappy and bored. One day, when there was no one in the house but me, I put the pistol to my head and held it there, loaded, a long time, and wondered if I would be any happier if I were to pull the trigger. But then, I began to think, if I do, I might miss something. I haven't been to the ranch yet, nor to the top of the volcano, nor to the bullfights in Mexico, nor graduated from high school, nor got married. So I put the pistol down and went back to my bookkeeping.

The Big Sea, 46–47

Langston Hughes dreamed of his absent father and at last was able to join him in Mexico. Unfortunately, the expectations Hughes had built were unrealistic. He grew increasingly lonely. All who have read Langston Hughes's poetry and other writings are thankful that he put down the pistol on that lonely day in Mexico.

The black period through which most travelers pass does not last very long, and when the beast is dead we look back from a happier vantage point and wonder why we felt so endangered.

 Have you had times of feeling sorry for yourself? Can you identify why? Was it in part the result of disappointed expectations?

 Curiosity about life and the thirst for new adventure helped Hughes overcome the beasts he faced. What or who helped you slay your beasts?

JAMES BOSWELL

Dr. Samuel Johnson's character, religious, moral, political, and literary, nay his figure and manner, are, I believe, more generally known than those of almost any man; yet it may not be superfluous here to attempt a sketch of him. Let my readers then remember that he was a sincere and zealous Christian, of high church of England and monarchical principles, which he would not tamely suffer to be questioned; steady and inflexible in maintaining the obligations of piety and virtue, both from a regard to the order of society, and from a veneration for the Great Source of all order; correct, nay stern in his taste; hard to please, and easily offended, impetuous and irritable in his temper, but of a most humane and benevolent heart; having a mind stored with a vast and various collection of learning and knowledge, which he communicated with peculiar perspicuity and force, in rich and choice expression. He united a most logical head with a most fertile imagination, which gave him an extraordinary advantage in arguing; for he could reason close or wide, as he saw best for the moment. He could, when he chose it, be the greatest sophist that ever wielded a weapon in the schools of declamation; but he indulged this only in conversation; for he owned he sometimes talked for victory; he was too conscientious to make errour permanent and pernicious, by deliberately writing it. He was conscious of his superiority. He loved praise when it was brought to him; but was too proud to seek for it. He was somewhat susceptible of flattery. His mind was so full of imagery, that he might have been perpetually a poet. It has been often remarked, that in his poetical pieces, which it is to be regretted are so few, because so excellent, his style is easier than in his prose. There is deception in this: it is not easier, but better suited to the dignity of verse; as one may dance with grace, whose motions, in ordinary walking, — in the common step, are awkward. He had a constitutional melancholy, the clouds of which darkened the brightness of his fancy, and gave a gloomy cast to his whole course of thinking: yet, though grave and awful in his deportment, when he thought it necessary or proper, — he frequently indulged himself in pleasantry and sportive sallies. He was prone to superstition, but not to credulity. Though his imagination might incline him to a belief of the marvellous, and the mysterious, his vigorous reason examined the evidence with jealousy. He had a loud voice, and a slow deliberate utterance, which no doubt gave some additional weight to the sterling metal of his conversation. Lord Pembroke said once to me at Wilton, with a happy pleasantry, and some truth, that "Dr. Johnson's sayings would not appear so extraordinary, were it not for his *bow-wow way.*"

A Journal of a Tour to the Hebrides with Samuel Johnson, 6–8

Assuming the accuracy of James Boswell's description of Samuel Johnson, what do you think in Johnson's character and temperament will aid or hinder his learning about and interpreting Scotland? (After you have answered, turn to page 234 in Stage X: Discovering the Boon, and read the Samuel Johnson excerpt. You may be surprised at what you find.)

 What do you see in your study abroad and service-learning companions that may help or hinder their progress of learning and of rendering service? Will you lead or be led by them? Have you felt any need to stand apart from the group? Why?

JANE ADDAMS

The long illness left me in a state of nervous exhaustion with which I struggled for years, traces of it remaining long after Hull-House was opened in 1889. At the best it allowed me but a limited amount of energy, so that doubtless there was much nervous depression at the foundation of the spiritual struggles which this chapter is forced to record. However, it could not have been all due to my health, for as my wise little notebook sententiously remarked, "In his own way each man must struggle, lest the moral law become a far-off abstraction utterly separated from his active life."

It would, of course, be impossible to remember that some of these struggles ever took place at all, were it not for these selfsame notebooks, in which, however, I no longer wrote in moments of high resolve, but judging from the internal evidence afforded by the books themselves, only in moments of deep depression when overwhelmed by a sense of failure.

Twenty Years at Hull-House, 48–49

Jane Addams's struggles with her health and with accompanying depression was linked to her spiritual and moral struggles.

 What beasts have you battled—loneliness, confusion, exhaustion? Have they influenced your view of yourself and the world?

 Have your struggles helped in the clarification of your values? Have they increased your understanding of and empathy for others who are suffering?

 When are you most likely to want to write in your journal? In times of exhilaration, quiet reflection, or discouragement?

In her journal, Jane Addams named a beast: "Each man [person] must struggle, lest the moral law become a far-off abstraction utterly separated from his active life."

 Can you cite examples from your study of the history and literature of your host nation in which the moral law was separate from action? Have you seen this human tendency and temptation in your service agency? In yourself?

Sana Hasan

A howl greeted the lunch bell. The women jostled past me, stampeding through the open door and down the staircase; in a flash the room had emptied. For myself, as for the others who rushed toward the dining room, the chairs were a far greater attraction than the food.

I tried to keep tabs on the vanishing trail of plastic aprons, but in vain. The last one shot through the revolving door, and I found myself on the second floor, abandoned by all. I opened one or two doors but found no trace of a dining room. Just then, a man with a giant torso and a small, egg-shaped head came out of the bathroom. I asked him where the dining room was.

Flashing his gold tooth in an insinuating smile, he led me with many gallant flourishes of his hand toward a door, which he held open for me. I stepped inside an immense work hall, and before I had time to focus my somewhat dazed eyes on the mountains of chicken carcasses that lay about, I found myself lying atop a bed of crushed ice, smothered by an avalanche of hot, sticky kisses that descended down my neck and throat. How I would ever have extracted myself from under this load I cannot say, for it is certain that no matter how much I hollered, no one would have heard me. But as chance would have it, Shaul, the Moroccan rabbi who was in charge of the salination of the chickens in accordance with Jewish religious law, happened to walk by. Hard as it was to believe, my three-hundred-pound assailant turned white at the sight of this mere gnome of a man. I did not linger long enough to see what ensued.

Halfway down the corridor, I met a woman who pointed me in the direction of the dining room. I went down one more flight of stairs, pushed open a door, and almost fell into the arms of my supervisor. I told her indignantly what had happened. "That must have been Krysztof," she said, and burst out laughing. Then, pointing out a slender, middle-aged woman with wispy gray hair at a table across the room, she whispered to me that he was her husband.

"What?" I exclaimed, shocked. "You mean his wife works here, and he behaves like that?"

"Oh, don't take it so seriously! He just likes to have some fun once in a while. All men are animals when it comes to sex. They can't help themselves. Why, I bet your husband would do the same thing if he had the chance," she said, winking at me.

"He most certainly wouldn't!" I asserted.

"Really?" she said, her eyes wide with astonishment. "Then he can't be much of a man!" Later, I discovered that the Georgians were the Latin lovers of the Soviet bloc; the male workers at the factory constantly boasted of their prowess, bragging that all Russian women vied for their favors and preferred them to their own husbands because of their passionate foreplay.

Enemy in the Promised Land, 132–133

The attitudes about relations between the sexes are among the most perplexing and disturbing for those living in another culture. Imagine Sana Hasan's indignation when her assault was treated so lightly!

 What has troubled, confused, frightened, angered, or amused you about the relations between men and women? How do local people interpret words or actions? Is there a class difference in their response? Is your host culture changing its sexual mores? Have your attitudes changed in any way?

OCTAVIO PAZ

We are witnessing now, at the end of the century, the resurrection of ethnic and psychic passions, beliefs, ideas, and realities that seemed to have been long buried. The return of religious passion and nationalist fervor hides an ambiguous meaning: Is it the return of ghosts and demons that reason had exorcised, or is it the revelation of profound truths and realities that had been ignored by our proud intellectual constructs? It is not easy to answer this question. What can be said is that the revival of nationalism and fundamentalism—why don't they call it by its true name, fanaticism?—has become a great threat to international peace and the integrity of nations. In India, this threat is permanent and daily. I have said that the solution is double: secularism and democracy. The task is particularly difficult because it requires a delicate balance between federalism and centralism. Luckily, although Hindu fanaticism is strong in the north, in Maharashtra and certain other regions, it is weak in the south. I believe that heterogeneity will work in favor of secularism and against the hegemonic pretensions of Hinduism.

In Light of India, 132–133

Octavio Paz recognizes two possible explanations of current religious and political zealotry.

 Have you seen examples of this in your host country? In your home country? What might be its cause in each place?

 Paz posits secularism and democracy as the solutions for "this threat to international peace." Do you agree? Can you give an example of how secularism or democracy has helped or hindered the development of peaceful relations in your community?

 What have you learned about federalism and centralism in your host nation? Why does Paz say a delicate balance is required?

 Are you of the same religion as most people in your host nation, or a different one? How do people view you as a result of your religion? How do you view them?

STAGE VII

PASSING THROUGH THE GATES

A succession of gates marks the progress of the hero's journey. The passage through each is a milestone, with the gate ahead viewed as the next obstacle and the one behind as a step of accomplishment in reaching the destination.

Some gates in a hero's passage are wide and welcoming, and the traveler passes through with relative ease. But other gates are guarded by strong and sometimes fierce creatures with the power to determine who may cross over to the other side. (Here guardian spirits and mentors can be useful.)

Like Odysseus, confronted by the narrow passage between the rock of Scylla and the whirlpool of Charybdis, so other travelers have been stopped in their journeys by these symbolic gates.

The gates of the hero's story are metaphors for markers on the interior road to understanding. We must ask what ideas, assumptions, attitudes, and behaviors act as gatekeepers preventing our reaching a higher level of appreciation of another culture and of ourselves. Which of these give way graciously, allowing us to proceed on the road ahead and which are unyielding?

SANA HASAN

Our apartment, on the exclusive residential island of Zamalek, had one of the finest views in Cairo. Our veranda overlooked the Nile. On a crisp, cool day, one could hear the palm trees swish in the breeze, their branches brushing against the window panes. Behind them, the simple, lean hulls of feluccas glided gracefully over the water. White sails dipped and rose in the wind. Sometimes a flock of birds would hover overhead with outstretched wings flashing and gleaming in the sunlight.

It was not by mere coincidence that my family lived on an island—a situation I always saw as an apt metaphor for our social insularity.

Two bridges linked the small island of Zamalek to the mainland. One of them, the Boulak, which our chauffeur had instructions to avoid, led to the poor section of town. There life had hardly ever changed. The alleyways teemed with street vendors: wizened, bleary-eyed men in *kaffiyehs,* carting *sus,* a licorice syrup; little boys with pinched cheeks and bad teeth peddling sugar cane; black-veiled women balancing urns of buffalo milk on their heads.

It was a world we hardly knew outside of the organ grinders who came to beg for money under our windows. Father would toss them a coin, in exchange for which their monkeys would perform a few grateful somersaults. And Mother would shake her head, saying, *"C'est une honte! Le gouvernement devrait ramasser ces espèces et les mettre hors de vue."* ("It's a shame! The government should collect those specimens [of humanity] and put them out of sight.")

Enemy in the Promised Land, 10–11

Sana Hasan describes how her wealthy family sheltered her from the realities of the poor in her own country of Egypt. For those so sheltered, relating directly to the poor or to those with other needs can be a difficult passage.

 What was your experience before entering the service-learning program? Were you protected from direct encounters with the poor, the elderly, the disabled, or any other group?

 How did you feel when you first saw and then had to interact with those whom your agency serves?

 Are you able to identify any milestones in your passage that mark a breakthrough in your ability to communicate and relate on a new and deeper level with those whose circumstances are different from yours?

JANE ADDAMS

For the following weeks I went about London almost furtively, afraid to look down narrow streets and alleys lest they disclose again this hideous human need and suffering. I carried with me for days at a time that curious surprise we experience when we first come back into the streets after days given over to sorrow and death; we are bewildered that the world should be going on as usual and unable to determine which is real, the inner pang or the outward seeming. In time all huge London came to seem unreal save the poverty in its East End. During the following two years on the continent, while I was irresistibly drawn to the poorer quarters of each city, nothing among the beggars of South Italy nor among the saltminers of Austria carried with it the same conviction of human wretchedness which was conveyed by this momentary glimpse of an East London street. It was, of course, a most fragmentary and lurid view of the poverty of East London, and quite unfair. I should have been shown either less or more, for I went away with no notion of the hundreds of men and women who had gallantly identified their fortunes with these empty-handed people, and who, in church and chapel, "relief works," and charities, were at least making an effort towards its mitigation.

Twenty Years at Hull-House, 50

Sometimes first impressions are so strong that they dominate our ability to see a culture in a balanced way. First impressions may come directly, as in the first days of a new situation, or they may come from a powerful book or movie. Jane Addams, concerned as she was with the poor and feeling so deeply their plight, reports seeing all through the lens of the suffering.

 Has one memorable moment dominated — and perhaps skewed — your perspective?

 Have you any concern that has dominated your view of your host culture to the exclusion of other dimensions? Has your view changed as you have learned more?

 Addams believed that she "should have been shown less or more." Have you ever traveled or volunteered in a way that you later realized was too little for understanding the true situation? Have you, in your program of service-learning, seen and experienced too little or too much of any one part of the culture to have a balanced and accurate picture?

James Boswell

[Johnson's] prejudice against Scotland was announced almost as soon as he began to appear in the world of letters. In his *London*, a poem, are the following nervous lines:

> For who would leave, unbribed, Hibernia's land?
> Or change the rocks of Scotland for the Strand?
> There none are swept by sudden fate away;
> But all, whom hunger spares, with age decay.

The truth is, like the ancient Greeks and Romans, he allowed himself to look upon all nations but his own as barbarians: not only Hibernia, and Scotland, but Spain, Italy, and France, are attacked in the same poem. If he was particularly prejudiced against the Scots, it was because they were more in his way; because he thought their success in England rather exceeded the due proportion of their real merit; and because he could not but see in them that nationality which I believe no liberal-minded Scotsman will deny. He was indeed, if I may be allowed the phrase, at bottom much of a John Bull; much of a blunt "true born Englishman". There was a stratum of common clay under the rock of marble....

I am, I flatter myself, completely a citizen of the world. In my travels through Holland, Germany, Switzerland, Italy, Corsica, France, I never felt myself from home; and I sincerely love "every kindred and tongue and people and nation". I subscribe to what my late truly learned and philosophical friend Mr. Crosbie said, that the English are better animals than the Scots; they are nearer the sun: their blood is richer, and more mellow: but when I humour any of them in an outrageous contempt of Scotland, I fairly own I treat them as children. And thus I have, at some moments, found myself obliged to treat even Dr. Johnson.

To Scotland however he ventured; and he returned from it in great humour, with his prejudices much lessened, and with very grateful feelings of the hospitality with which he was treated; as is evident from that admirable work, his *Journey to the Western Islands of Scotland.*

> *A Journal of a Tour to the Hebrides with Samuel Johnson,* 6–7

James Boswell claims that for him the passage from one culture into another was easy, but that for Samuel Johnson it was much more difficult. Perhaps it was because Johnson was so much older than Boswell, or that Johnson began with such strong opinions, set before he had direct experience. But Johnson's prejudices gave way because of his powers of observation and his willingness to reflect honestly on what he saw.

 What prejudgments, either harsh or favorable, have given way for you as your experience of the host culture lengthens and deepens?

Boswell describes in educated and urbane Johnson an odd kind of reasoning: "he thought their [the Scots] success rather exceeded the due portion of their real merit."

 Have you read or heard others voice a similar opinion about the people of your host nation? Have you had such thoughts yourself?

 Has your study, service, and experience of living in your host culture altered your view? In which direction?

OCTAVIO PAZ

Years ago, walking with a foreign friend who had recently arrived in Mexico City, I showed him one of our most beautiful avenues, the Paseo de la Reforma. He looked at me in surprise and said, "But Mexico is a Catholic country." I had to explain to him that the word "Reforma" does not refer to the religious revolution of Luther and Calvin that changed the world, but rather to some laws created by President Benito Juárez in the last century. Similarly, in our National School of Anthropology, the phrase "Western culture" does not refer to the civilization of Europe but to a relatively primitive pre-Hispanic group in the northwest of Mexico.

All this would be funny were it not frightening. Nationalism is not a jovial god: it is Moloch drunk with blood.

In Light of India, 126

Leaping to interpretation based on one's own culture and with too little knowledge of the host culture poses an obstacle for almost every traveler-hero at one time or another along the road.

 Have you had such an experience?

 If your misperception was known to others, what was their response? And what was your reaction when you realized your mistake? Was the incident harmless, embarrassing, amusing, or hurtful? Who or what corrected your misperception?

 What might remain uncorrected? For example, have you missed the humor when others have laughed? Might you have misunderstood what they were laughing about?

Octavio Paz says that misinterpretation based on our own cultural knowledge and ignorance of others "would be funny were it not frightening. Nationalism is not a jovial god: it is Moloch drunk with blood."

 Cite examples from the history of your host or home nation to support Paz's statement.

 What consequences might you imagine if most people in your home nation were to see your host nation only through the lens of their own values? Or if your host nation were to see your home nation only through its values and beliefs?

 How might education be constructed to minimize such mis-understandings? How has the combination of study and service contributed or failed to contribute to your ability to see your host nation directly rather than from the vantage of your own culture?

 How might you help, when you return home, to correct mis-perceptions of your fellow citizens or your government about your host country?

KATHLEEN NORRIS

"Extremes," John R. Milton suggests in his history of South Dakota, is "perhaps the key word for Dakota...What happens to extremes is that they come together, and the result is a kind of tension." I make no attempt in this book to resolve the tensions and contradictions I find in the Dakotas between hospitality and insularity, change and inertia, stability and instability, possibility and limitation, between hope and despair, between open hearts and closed minds.

I suspect that these are the ordinary contradictions of human life, and that they are so visible in Dakota because we are so few people living in a stark landscape.

Dakota: A Spiritual Geography, 7

Strangers in a foreign land find that the gates to sophisticated appreciation of the culture are blocked by their own monolithic views. Gaining passage through the gates requires recognition of the complexities and contradictions of a culture.

 Before you arrived and in the first days and weeks in your host country, did you have a single and simplistic view of the country? What experiences have you had that have made you appreciate the variety within your host culture? Of what contrasts and contradictions have you become aware through direct experience or from your study of history and culture?

 Has your view of yourself become more complex? Are your own contradictory purposes, ideas, and feelings paralyzing or are they a source of vitality?

ANTHONY WINKLER

One day on a visit to Montego Bay I was standing and gazing nostalgically at the house in which I had spent most of my boyhood years when a higgler woman and her young grandson who were selling fruit nearby spoke to me. I walked over and we began to talk. Her grandson looked up at me defiantly when I said that I had spent much of my childhood in that house across the street.

"You saying you a Jamaican?" he asked suspiciously.

I said that I was.

His lips curled with contempt.

"You not a Jamaican," he said.

"I was born in Kingston Public Hospital,"I said angrily. "I went to Cornwall College right here in Montego Bay. I lived in that house for seven years."

"You not a Jamaican," he repeated stubbornly. "You a white man."

This was too much to bear in front of the very house in which I had spent so much of my childhood.

"I'm a rass claat Jamaican!" I snapped.

"Lawd Jesus God, sah," the old woman wailed, "Beg you! No cuss no bad word in me old ear."

The boy was unmoved. "Any white man can learn bad word from book," he said scornfully.

"De gentleman is a Jamaican!" the old lady scolded. "Me could tell from me first set eye 'pon him. Hush up you mouth 'bout it."

But there was no convincing the boy. His grandmother lamented that he was a youth, and like all the youth of today had no manners, and she was sorry for his rudeness. It was a pinprick, and I no doubt made too much of it. But I was so enraged that I could have strangled the wretch with my bare hands and laughed about it afterwards.

Going Home to Teach, 76

Just as the hero may be stopped at the gates by his own assumptions, so may his passage to a new culture be barred by the cultural stereotypes of those in his host nation. Other excerpts in this section relate to the traveler's false assumptions; this one is of residents unable to accept the truth about a visitor. To know and to be known are both necessary for inclusion into a new community.

 What beliefs about you have been expressed by those in your host country? Are any a distortion of your true identity? What have you said or done to try to correct the image? Have you been successful?

KATHLEEN NORRIS

There are ... uncanny echoes of the Old South in the literary world, where it's always been more acceptable to be from the South than from South Dakota. In the 1980s, books set on the Plains, some by writers living there, began to receive regular mention in the *New York Times Book Review*. But the price of this acceptance may prove high. It's the mythologized Old South that's acceptable to readers outside that region, and this may prove true for Dakota as well. We could be facing a situation like that of Native Americans who came to be seen as romantic while their culture was being destroyed. Indian children were punished for speaking their own language, but Indian words and symbols were appropriated to sell a myth of freedom on the American road. Pontiac, Cherokee, even the sacred Thunderbird.

I watched uneasily as a "Dakota chic" surfaced in America in the mid-80s, in both tony urban restaurants and national advertising campaigns. Dakota Beer came on the market in 1986 with ads focused on "wheat from the heartland and the people who grow it." The ads were filmed in Montana, but as one South Dakota official put it, with typical self-effacement, "at least they came to within a state of us." That same year, Lee Iacocca, wearing a white cowboy hat, introduced the Dodge Dakota pickup truck, and the corporation flew real Dakota cowboys and Indians to Hollywood to pose for ads. It's ironic that in the year the beer came out, the *Rapid City Journal* reported that over 20 percent of South Dakota's farmers, the good folk growing that wheat, either left or seriously contemplated leaving their land for economic reasons, and so many auto and farm implement dealers closed their doors that people would have had to drive a hundred miles or more to buy the truck, if they could afford it. That year, in the 576xx Zip Code area, the median household income was $15,670. (Currently it stands at $17,660.)

Dakota: A Spiritual Geography, 29–30

Romantic and idealized notions of a place and people may be as false as negative stereotypes, and stand in the way of true understanding. In their distortion of truth, such ideas are only another way of failing to do honor to a people and culture.

 What romantic images have you had that you later revised? What have you learned from the history, literature, and culture of your hosts and of your own culture that gave rise to these false notions? What study, experiences, and people have helped you to unlock gates leading to a more honest judgment?

Emily Bronson Conger

As between Chinese and Japanese, for fidelity, honesty, veracity and uprightness, my impression is largely in favor of the Chinese as a race. Captain Finch told me that on this ship, the Gælic, over which he had had charge for the past fifteen years, he had had, as head waiter, the same Chinaman that he started out with, and in all this period of service he never had occasion to question the integrity of this most faithful servant, who in the entire time had not been absent from the ship more than three days in all. On these rare occasions, this capable man had left for his substitute such minute instructions on bits of rice paper, placed where needed, that the work was carried on smoothly without need of supervision or other direction. The same holds true of Chinese servants on our Pacific coast. I was much pleased with the attention they gave each and every one of us during the entire trip; it was better service than any that I have ever seen on Atlantic ships. In the whole month's trip, I never heard one word of complaint.

An Ohio Woman in the Philippines, 32

Emily Conger begins her voyage to the Philippines making judgments about Asians on the basis of very little information. In this passage she decides in favor of the Chinese and against the entire nation of Japan on the basis of one Chinese man — and the story of his worthiness is secondhand! The gates to understanding remained barred for her until she learned to suspend judgment and await more extensive observation on which to draw conclusions.

 Have you heard others stating categorical conclusions after very little experience? Have you yourself made such judgments? Have you later revised these opinions after having additional information and experience?

LANGSTON HUGHES

On the way back to the ranch, my father suddenly announced that he had made up his mind to have me study mining engineering.

"In another five or six years," he said, "these mines will be open and there will be plenty of work for you here, near the ranch."

"But I can't be a mining engineer, I'm no good at mathematics," I said, as we walked the horses.

"You can learn anything you put your mind to," my father said. "And engineering is something that will make you some money. What do you want to do, live like a nigger all your life? Look at your mother, waiting table in a restaurant! Don't you want to get anywhere?"

"Sure," I said. "But I don't want to be a mining engineer."

"What do you want to be?"

"I don't know. But I think a writer."

"A writer?" my father said. "A writer? Do they make money?"

"Some of them do, I guess."

"I never heard of a colored one that did," said my father.

"Alexandre Dumas," I answered.

"Yes, but he was in Paris, where they don't care about color. That's what I want you to do, Langston. Learn something you can make a living from anywhere in the world, in Europe or South America, and don't stay in the States, where you have to live like a nigger with niggers."

"But I like Negroes," I said. "We have plenty of fun."

"Fun!" my father shouted. "How can you have fun with the color line staring you in the face? I never could."

We were riding in a bowl of pine trees, with the distant rim of the mountains all around and the sky very blue. For once, my father did not seem to be in a hurry. He let his horse mosey along, biting at the wayside grass. As we rode, my father outlined a plan he had made up in his mind for me, a plan that I had never dreamed of before. He wanted me to go to Switzerland to college, perhaps to Basle, or one of the cantons where one could learn three languages at once, French, German, and Italian, directly from the people. Then he wanted me to go to a German engineering school. Then come back to live in Mexico.

The thought of trigonometry, physics, and chemistry in a *foreign* language was more than I could bear. In English, they were difficult enough. But as a compromise to Switzerland and Germany, I suggested Columbia [University] in New York—mainly because I wanted to see Harlem.

The Big Sea, 61–62

A wonderful writer would have been lost to the world had Langston Hughes followed his father's advice and become an engineer. Sometimes the goals we set for ourselves are either limiting or unrealistic and so impede the progress of the journey. At other times, it is the aspirations of others that lock the gates for heroes and prevent their finding their own vocation.

 Have others tried to prevent your passage by seeking to impose on you their own beliefs about the world and their own idea of the direction your life journey should take?

 Have the opinions of others prevented any group in your host culture from developing?

 Have you met an individual served by your agency whom you believe has unrealized potential? What do you believe is your responsibility in such a case? Would your supervisor agree?

PAUL COWAN

The day before my graduation with the class of 1963, Medgar Evers was murdered by Byron de La Beckwith. I heard about it as I was driving to meet my parents at Logan Airport. I was ashamed that I'd spend the next day in sunny Harvard Yard, hearing speaker after speaker praise the university and the nation. They should mourn. They should put themselves on trial; they were accomplices in the crime of segregation.

For a moment I considered asking my parents to return to New York while I flew down to bloody Mississippi. I would confront the state, hands on hips, chin sticking out (sweat dripping from my reddened face, horn-rimmed glasses skidding from my nose); I would praise free speech in full voice, bellow its glory throughout the land. What an appropriate commencement that would be! The best possible way to begin my life in the adult world.

But my parents had been waiting a long time for me to graduate. They wanted to see me receive my diploma, and I had to admit that the part of me that had been battling Harvard wanted to participate in the ceremonial triumph. Besides, I didn't know anyone in Mississippi. What would I do once I got there?

So I rewrote an editorial I had published in the *Crimson* three months before, when William Moore was assassinated during his lonely hike to Alabama. I told the Americans who happened to be gathered in Cambridge that festive week that their moral nerve would decay unless they responded at once to the atrocities that were occurring with increasing regularity in the Southern states; and those who knew me praised my prose style (they didn't realize that I had cribbed the metaphor from Norman Mailer) and my courage for publishing such bold opinions.

I was a Harvard pundit that year. People regarded me as an authority, and I was proud to act as one. It was a fleeting

175

experience, but it did me enormous harm. A dissenter gained respect too easily at Harvard College during John Kennedy's short administration. He became confident of his opinions much too early. It was a sure way to acquire very bad habits.

The Making of an Un-American, 26–27

Paul Cowan says that as a dissenter he gained respect too easily and became confident of his opinions too early.

 Do you agree that early affirmation may act as a gate preventing passage to the next level of understanding? Have you seen or perhaps yourself experienced more praise than you deserved? How has it affected your struggle with the hard questions of life?

One advantage of moving into a new community at any stage of life, but especially as a young adult, is the opportunity it affords to shed your past. In a new situation you are living with people who know nothing of your previous success or failure.

 Is there congruence between the reputation you have among family, friends, and professors at home and the reputation you are developing in your host community? Are you in any way re-defining yourself?

JANE ADDAMS

I remember a happy busy mother who, complacent with the knowledge that her daughter daily devoted four hours to her music, looked up from her knitting to say, "If I had had your opportunities when I was young, my dear, I should have been a very happy girl. I always had musical talent, but such training as I had, foolish little songs and waltzes and not time for half an hour's practice a day."

The mother did not dream of the sting her words left and that the sensitive girl appreciated only too well that her opportunities were fine and unusual, but she also knew that in spite of some facility and much good teaching she had no genuine talent and never would fulfill the expectations of her friends. She looked back upon her mother's girlhood with positive envy because it was so full of happy industry and extenuating obstacles, with undisturbed opportunity to believe that her talents were unusual. The girl looked wistfully at her mother, but had not the courage to cry out what was in her heart: "I might believe I had unusual talent if I did not know what good music was; I might enjoy half an hour's practice a day if I were busy and happy the rest of the time. You do not know what life means when all the difficulties are removed! I am simply smothered and sickened with advantages. It is like eating a sweet dessert the first thing in the morning."

This, then, was the difficulty, this sweet dessert in the morning and the assumption that the sheltered, educated girl has nothing to do with the bitter poverty and the social maladjustment which is all about her, and which, after all, cannot be concealed, for it breaks through poetry and literature in a burning tide which overwhelms her; it peers at her in the form of heavy-laden market women and underpaid street laborers, gibing her with a sense of her uselessness.

Twenty Years at Hull-House, 52–53

The hero approaching the gates which open to the next stage of the journey must pass by strong creatures who jealously guard the portals. Some guardians of the gates are well-meaning and love the hero dearly, but still prevent her passage by their very acts of protection. Showering on the traveler every comfort — which they call opportunity — these guardians actually stand in the way of true accomplishment which comes from meeting a challenge.

 Do you understand Jane Addams's young friend who envied her mother's childhood for its "extenuating obstacles?"

 Do your family, friends, and teachers want your life to be easier than you need or want it to be? Is your choosing service-learning abroad in any way a desire for a rigorous test of your abilities and perseverance? In what ways has your college made education too easy for you?

 Have others pushed upon you ambitions that you know are inappropriate to your skills and interests?

 Did people understand your wanting to serve as part of your study abroad or, in their concern, did they try to guard the gates of your passage? Have they encouraged you to ignore the pain that is all around you, as did the mother of the music student about whom Jane Addams wrote?

MARY KINGSLEY

They are talking of making Buea into a sanatorium for the fever-stricken. I do not fancy somehow that it's a suitable place for a man who has got all the skin off his nerves with fever and quinine, and is very liable to chill; but all Governments on the Coast, English, German, or French, are stark mad on the subject of sanatoriums in high places, though the experience they have had of them has clearly pointed out that they are valueless in West Africa, and a man's one chance is to get out to sea on a ship that will take him outside the three-mile-deep fever-belt of the coast.

Travels in West Africa, 604

All the other Protestant missions are following the Basel Mission's lead, and, recognising that a good deal of their failure arises from a want of this practical side in their instruction, are now starting technical schools: — the Church of England in Sierra Leone, the Wesleyans on the Gold Coast, and the Presbyterians in Calabar.

In some of these technical schools the sort of instruction given is, to my way of thinking, ill-advised; arts of no immediate or great use in the present culture-condition of West Africa — such as printing, book-binding, and tailoring — being taught. But this is not the case under the Wesleyans, who also teach smith's work, carpentering, bricklaying, waggon-building, &c. Alas! None of the missions save the Roman Catholic teach the thing that it is most important the natives should learn, in the face of the conditions that European government of the Coast has induced, namely, improved methods of agriculture, and plantation work.

Travels in West Africa, 28–29

The Spanish authorities insist that the natives who come into the town should have something on, and so they array themselves in a bit of cotton cloth, which before they are out of sight of the town on their homeward way, they strip off and stuff into their baskets, showing in this, as well as in all other particulars, how uninfluencible by white culture they are.

Travels in West Africa, 57

It is not unusual to find that the people in authority, sometimes from the best of motives, set up programs based on false premises. Those in authority may be foreign to the geography or local customs as were those cited by Mary Kingsley, or they may simply be of a different class or circumstance from those they serve.

 Have you observed or learned about programs that you believe are not very useful or even detrimental, blocking passage for the people they are meant to serve? What caused the errors in judgment?

 Have you seen any examples of people appearing to comply, but immediately reverting to traditional practice the minute they were beyond they rule of the authority? (If your work is with children, you undoubtedly have many examples, for children are masters of resistance!)

 What approaches on the part of the service agency with which you are working have hindered or helped you in being truly useful to the community you came to serve? What local beliefs and values should, in your opinion, be left alone and which should be challenged and toward what ends?

 Have you changed your mind in the course of the program about what is needed and what should or should not be done for your new community or the clients of your service agency?

STAGE VIII

RECOGNIZING GUIDES AND GUARDIAN SPIRITS

When the hero is most threatened, the challenges too great for his strength or ability, the dragons breathing fire and the gates firmly locked, there materialize in the story mentors or guardian spirits to come to his aid. As if by magic they appear, leading the way, blazing the trail, whispering the clue, handing over the secret weapon, delivering the key, and sometimes even giving their lives to save the hero in his hour of need.

Oh, the variety of forms these mentors, guides, and guardians assume in story and in real life! The fairy godmother, old hermit, clever monkey, shining angel, virginal maiden, knight errant, humble woodcutter, and little child are but a few of the guises these saviors take.

In some hero's tales, the mentors and guides are undeniable, coming in radiant light. But in other legends, they are like little elves darting in and out of the trees, seen one minute and hidden the next. Some are in disguise and are only later recognized to be the saviors that they are. And there is the occasional wolf in sheep's clothing—one decked out as a guardian angel but who is, in fact, a sorcerer, a tempter or a demon, leading the hero down a wrong and dangerous path.

But what comfort true mentors and guardians bring to the hero who discovers that on this otherwise solitary path she is not alone! Before and behind, above and below are those who know the road already, who possess the knowledge and wisdom to help the hero complete the journey successfully, and who stand ready and willing to guide the way.

Emily Bronson Conger

If I have any courage I owe it to my grandmother. I will perhaps be pardoned if I say that all my girlhood life was spent with my Grandmother Bronson, a very small women, weighing less than ninety pounds, small featured, always quaintly dressed in the old-fashioned Levantine silk with two breadths only in the skirt, a crossed silk handkerchief with a small white one folded neatly across her breast, a black silk apron, dainty cap made of sheer linen lawn with full ruffles. She it was who entered into all my child life and who used to tell me of her early pioneer days, and of her wonderful experiences with the Indians. In the War of 1812, fearing for his little family, my grandfather started her back to Connecticut on horse back with her four little children, the youngest, my father, only six months old. The two older children walked part of the way; whoever rode had to carry the baby and the next smallest child rode on a pillion that tied to the saddle. In this way she accomplished the long journey from Cleveland, Ohio, to Connecticut. When she used to tell me of the wonderful things that happened on this tedious journey, that took weeks and weeks to accomplish, I used to wonder if I should ever take so long a trip....

While my dear little grandmother dreaded the Indians, I did the treacherous Filipinos; while she dreaded the wolves, bears and wild beasts, I did the stab of the ever ready bolo and stealthy natives, and the prospect of fire; she endured the pangs of hunger, so did I; and I now feel that I am worthy to be her descendant and to sit by her side.

An Ohio Woman in the Philippines, 161–162

Emily Conger was in the Philippines at the time of American occupation. The movement to independence made inevitable conflict with and sometimes violence against Americans — thus her fear of one element in Philippine society.

Not all mentors are met on the journey. Some, like Emily Conger's grandmother, come from the hero's past. From the example set by her grandmother, Emily found the courage to face danger and overcome her fears.

 Who in your life instilled in you by word or example the values and qualities that now guide you on your journey?

 In the nation where you are studying and in the community in which you are serving, are there people who are revered for the example they have set?

JANE ADDAMS

Of the many things written of my father in that sad August in 1881, when he died, the one I cared for most was written by an old political friend of his who was then editor of a great Chicago daily. He wrote that while there were doubtless many members of the Illinois legislature who during the great contracts of the war time and the demoralizing reconstruction days that followed, had never accepted a bribe, he wished to bear testimony that he personally had known but this one man who had never been offered a bribe because bad men were instinctively afraid of him.

I feel now the hot chagrin with which I recalled this statement during those early efforts of Illinois in which Hull-House joined, to secure the passage of the first factory legislation. I was told by the representatives of an informal association of manufacturers that if the residents of Hull-House would drop this nonsense about a sweat shop bill, of which they knew nothing, certain business men would agree to give fifty thousand dollars within two years to be used for any of the philanthropic activities of the Settlement. As the fact broke upon me that I was being offered a bribe, the shame was enormously increased by the memory of this statement. What had befallen the daughter of my father that such a thing could happen to her? The salutary reflection that it could not have occurred unless a weakness in myself had permitted it, withheld me at least from an heroic display of indignation before the two men making the offer, and I explained as gently as I could that we had no ambition to make Hull-House "the largest institution on the West Side."

Twenty Years at Hull-House, 27–28

Jane Addams's hero and mentor was her father, who had educated her, guided her, and imparted his own high moral values to her.

 Is a member of your family a hero and guide for you? Do you ever, like Addams, feel you cannot live up to the high standards set for you?

 Is your participation in service-learning the expression of a family tradition of scholarship, service, or international and intercultural interests, or are you striking out in a new direction?

MARY KINGSLEY

One by one I took my old ideas derived from books and thoughts based on imperfect knowledge and weighed them against the real life around me, and found them either worthless or wanting. The greatest recantation I had to make I made humbly before I had been three months on the Coast in 1893. It was of my idea of the traders. What I had expected to find them was a very different thing to what I did find them; and of their kindness to me I can never sufficiently speak, for on that voyage I was utterly out of touch with the governmental circles, and utterly dependent on the traders, and the most useful lesson of all the lessons I learnt on the West Coast in 1893 was that I could trust them. Had I not learnt this very thoroughly I could never have gone out again and carried out the voyage I give you a sketch of in this book.

Thanks to "the Agent," I have visited places I could never otherwise have seen; and to the respect and affection in which he is held by the native, I owe it that I have done so in safety. When I have arrived off his factory in a steamer or canoe, unexpected, unintroduced, or turned up equally unheralded out of the bush in a dilapidated state, he has always received me with that gracious hospitality which must have given him, under Coast conditions, very real trouble and inconvenience — things he could have so readily found logical excuses against entailing upon himself for the sake of an individual whom he had never seen before — whom he most likely would never see again — and whom it was no earthly profit to him to see then. He has bestowed himself — Allah only knows where — on his small trading vessels so that I might have his one cabin. He has fished me out of sea and fresh water with boat-hooks; he has continually given me good advice, which if I had only followed would have enabled me to keep out of water and any other sort of affliction; and although he holds the meanest opinion of my intellect for going to such a place as West Africa for beetles,

187

fishes and fetish, he has given me the greatest assistance in my work. The value of that work I pray you withhold judgment on, until I lay it before you in some ten volumes or so mostly in Latin. All I know that is true regarding West African facts, I owe to the traders; the errors are my own.

Travels in West Africa, 6–7

Help often comes from surprising places. Mary Kingsley had been told of the evils of the traders, yet they proved her most reliable source of information and her stalwart friends.

 Where did you expect to find mentors and guardian spirits? Where in fact have you found them? Describe one source of unexpected help and support you have experienced.

Kingsley seems to have charmed all who met her through her curiosity, humor, intelligence, and open-mindedness. One can imagine that the traders might have been less protective and less forthright with their information had she been a different sort of person.

 What qualities do you possess that call forth or hinder aid from guides and guardian spirits?

SANA HASAN

[When] they saw young Jews who, like myself, were aimlessly drifting about, they tried to bring them back to the true path. They would invite them home for coffee and seek to revive their interest in Judaism. More often than not they succeeded, and would then offer to have them spend the night or, if there was already a houseguest, find another home for them in the neighborhood. Such hosts were not hard to find, because it was considered a divine duty *(mitzvah)* in this Orthodox neighborhood to make a secular youth repent and embrace Orthodoxy. Guests were then asked to prolong their stay for a few days, and religious instruction would begin almost at once. A pair of scissors applied to a young man's long hair made for beautiful earlocks, and a girl would exchange her jeans for black stockings and a "decent" hemline. Then they would be channeled into Mount Zion Yeshiva (the only one in Israel to accept girls). Sometimes the girls would be kept on as household members to help out with chores and with the host family's often numerous children until suitable marriages with Orthodox youths could be worked out for them by a *shadchan*.

Judith proposed that I stay on in their house for a few days to discover the beauties of the religious life, for, while most of the missionary work in their neighborhood centered around the saving of young men, she herself believed in the importance of reeducating young women because of the vital role they played in raising the future generation.

Moments before she had revealed her motive to me, I had been about to tell her my real identity, but now I thought to myself, why not? Here at last was a chance to live the religious life, which I had so far witnessed only as an outsider. I stifled my scruples and accepted her offer. Judith and David were obviously elated and went out of their way to make me feel welcome. David drove me back to the Ulpan that evening and waited in the car while I got a few things and left word in the office that I would be absent for several days.

My initiation into Orthodox Judaism began the next morning.

Enemy in the Promised Land, 175

The intentions of a would-be mentor are sometimes transparent; at other times they are less easily discerned. And the mentor who might be a savior to one sojourner is for another an enslaver.

 Who has tried to convert you to a religious, political, or social point of view? By what means? How have you responded?

 Whom have you sought to convert, and to what opinion or ideology? For what purpose? What response have you had from the target of your persuasive efforts?

 Is there a widely-acknowledged mentor or guardian in your host community? An individual, political party, or even another nation? From your knowledge of the political and social circumstances, do you believe this person or group has been a true or false mentor? Why?

LANGSTON HUGHES

Maximiliano, the *mozo*, took care of the horses and the chickens, swept the patio and the corral, and saddled the horses for me or my father. He was a silent boy who spoke but little Spanish, his being an Indian language from the hills. He slept on a pile of sacks in the tool shed, so I asked my father why he didn't give Maximiliano a bed, since there were several old beds around.

He said: "Never give an Indian anything. He doesn't appreciate it."

But he was wrong about that. I gave Maximiliano my spare centavos and cigarettes, and we became very good friends. He taught me to ride a horse without saddle or stirrups, how to tell a badly woven serape from a good one, and various other things that are useful to know in that high valley beneath the white volcanos.

The Big Sea, 44

Teachers, parents, agency supervisors, religion, and great books are among the easily recognized mentors. But mentors come as well from unexpected quarters and from among the most humble.

 Has aid come to you from an unexpected source? Have there been those to whom you expected to give help who in fact have been your helpers? Who have been your teachers and guardians in your new community?

KATHLEEN NORRIS

You should have filled your gas tank in Aberdeen, especially if you're planning to travel after dark. For many years there was no gasoline available at night (except in the summer) between Aberdeen and Miles City, Montana, a distance of nearly four hundred miles. Currently there are two 24-hour stations in towns nearly 200 miles apart. On the last stretch, the 78 miles from Baker, Montana, to Miles City, there are no towns at all, just a spectacularly desolate moonscape of sagebrush. Farmers will usually give or sell a little gas to stranded travelers, and small-town police forces often have keys to the local service stations so they can sell you enough to get you on your way. But the message is clear: you're in the West now. Pay attention to your gas gauge. Pay attention, period.

Dakota: A Spiritual Geography, 151

The gas gauge, farmers, local policemen—these Kathleen Norris identifies as guardian spirits on the western plains. She might have added the weather reporters on radio and television and the cell phone as guardians to the winter traveler in the Dakotas. If these things and people are to be useful in battling the perils of the journey, we need to learn to recognize them and, as Norris cautions, we need to pay attention to them.

 What or who have you recognized as guardian spirits in your new land? Are there any whom you recognized too late to be of use? To what must you pay attention?

OCTAVIO PAZ

Gandhi's actions, both religious and political—which, in his case, cannot be separated—not only resolved a situation that had seemed hopeless; he turned it into a triumph. The extremists also united the religious and the political, but with Gandhi the point of the union was quite different: nonviolence and friendship with the other religious communities, particularly the Muslims. Contrary to the extremists, for Gandhi politics did not expropriate religion: religion humanized politics. The Gandhian religion was not that of the orthodoxy; it was a reform version acceptable to the masses because they approved of his personal conduct. Gandhi achieved what the moderates could not: establishing deep roots among the people, and at the same time demonstrating to the extremists that tolerance and nonviolence were not incompatible with perseverance and effectiveness. For the masses, Gandhi embodied a figure venerated by all Hindus: the ascetic who renounces the world; for political and practical minds, he was a man of action, capable of speaking both to the masses and with the authorities, skilled in negotiation and incorruptible in his principles.

This fusion of the religious and the political, of asceticism and pragmatism, is only one aspect of the startling concordance of contradictions that made Gandhi a unique figure. He was a traditional Hindu but also a Westerner. The influence of the West was profound and is clearly perceptible in his political thinking and in his religion, the two inseparable sides of his personality. His political actions were not founded on any Hindu tradition, but rather on the pacifism of Leo Tolstoy; his ideas of social reform are closer to Kropotkin than to the Laws of Manu; behind his idea of passive resistance lies Thoreau's "civil disobedience." His family was Vishnuite, and he himself was an ardent devotee of Vishnu, yet he read the *Bhagavad-Gita* in the English translation by Sir Edwin Arnold. In Gandhi, the

Jain tradition of nonviolence *(ahimsa)* was fused with the activism of a Tolstoy or a Thoreau. (In 1847, Thoreau went to jail rather than pay the taxes for the American war against Mexico.) Nonviolence in India has a double basis: one, political and ethical, which is Western; the other, religious, which is Jain.

In Light of India, 111–112

Gandhi was a mentor and indeed a guardian spirit to India and to the world. Octavio Paz describes how Gandhi, who had lived in England and South Africa, wove together his multicultural education and experience into ideas and behavior that served the cause of Indian independence and later was a model for the Civil Rights Movement in the United States and other areas of the world.

 Are there leaders who have been mentors and guardian spirits in your home or host nation whose leadership has come from such a weaving of traditions?

 How might you use the experience you have had through intercultural service-learning to advise or aid others at home or abroad?

ANTHONY WINKLER

When I first arrived in America I made the mistake of thinking that the people I worked for were idiots because they were so faltering and inept in their speech. My first job was as an insurance clerk working for a man who often groped for words, and when he couldn't find the right one, would use the expression "set-up" as a substitute. So he would ask me to look into the "set-up" of a certain policy, when he really wanted to know whether its coverage extended to a particular risk. He would send me into the back room to "set up" the files when he wanted them alphabetized. "What's the set-up?" could mean anything from "What happened while I was out of the office?" to "Where are you going for lunch?"

Accustomed to English managers who expressed themselves with bullying precision, I thought my American boss a hopeless nitwit. But he wasn't. He simply reflected the countrified manners and folksy diction he had acquired from a childhood lived on an Iowa farm. That he had risen from the cornfield to ownership of a major insurance brokerage in California was proof of his business shrewdness. He had a wonderful memory for details and was able to spew out nearly verbatim the exact coverage of a policy he had written ten years before. But his manners and speech gave absolutely no indication of his abilities or that he was a monied gentleman with a prosperous business in Pasadena and a mini-mansion in the ritzy suburb of San Marino.

After watching American leaders for some years now I am even convinced that many of them deliberately stumble in their speech because they think that doing so makes them sound more sincere than if they volubly said what they meant. A suspicion of smooth talking runs deep in the American character, making it smarter for the politician to hem and haw before his constituents and seem one of the boys than to unwittingly discomfit them with an invidious glibness.

I have often thought, too, that the American's reputation for practicality might in some obscure way be related to his distaste for class accoutrements. The upper-class colonial Englishman often tried to be squinting at the world dimly through the clutter of superstitions and protocol inherited by his membership in a privileged group. He seemed perpetually blundering about in a fog of rigidly correct English, etiquette, and a doltish worldview. In old movies we often see him standing stubbornly erect and in a heroically disciplined line on the battlefield just as he is about to be skewered in his red-coated belly by a Zulu spear. It never occurs to the fool to abandon his dignity and duck or lie flat. The American would assuredly have ducked, not because he is more cowardly, but because his mind is uncluttered enough by class codes and expectations to be practical.

That is why the American is today riding space shuttles while the Englishman is wondering how he happened to fall off his high horse.

The sad fact was that many of the tutors at our school, especially the older ones educated in Jamaica or England, struck me as out-and-out boobs. Many had only a smattering of understanding about their discipline. Many could not write a decent sentence if escaping the gallows required it, and many could only pass on in parrot fashion, what they themselves had been force-fed as students. The Englishman's rote learning had wreaked a terrible destruction on their minds while carving only a narrow slug's path through the mysteries of their disciplines. Here they inched forward in fear and dread that some precocious student would come along and knock them off the dimly lit track and into the surrounding darkness with a question.

Some of these elder ones annoyed me incessantly. I could not endure their sanctimoniousness, their standing on ceremony with students, their pompous air of dignity. I found myself bickering constantly with them, arguing against this and that idiotic classroom tradition.

Going Home to Teach, 208–209

Sometimes our own cultural conditioning prevents our recognizing a true mentor when we meet one.

 Have you at first dismissed someone who later proved to be a person of wisdom and experience who could serve as a mentor to you, as Anthony Winkler did his boss?

Society often elevates those to the role of mentor who, however unwittingly, work against the good of those they tutor and for whom they serve as role models. In Winkler's judgment many of the school teachers of Jamaica fit that description.

 Have you seen people in the role of mentor or guardian spirit who you believe are, at the least, not helpful and, at worst, destructive?

PAUL COWAN

That week Bob [Moses] became, for me, the embodiment of the America for which I had been searching.

His quiet modest personality was so compelling that many of us who hardly knew him strove to get close to him by imitating his manner. For example, his habit of sitting toward the back of the auditorium during important meetings: it was his way of forcing others to be leaders. Or his careful silences. When one asked Bob a question there was always a long pause before he answered, sometimes a pause of several minutes. He had been a math major at Hamilton College, a philosophy student in graduate school at Harvard. I had never met anyone who chose his words with such care, whose sentences were accordingly so lucid and precise. He told us once that he had decided that most people talk too much and that he would use words only when they were absolutely required. So he shared what he knew by example and not, like most of us, by making long speeches or issuing orders.

His actions showed me my own hypocrisy. Someone who had known Moses while he was still a schoolteacher in New York told me that the year before Bob went to Mississippi he had spent a great deal of time listening to old Odetta records. He would play them over and over, night after night. Well, Odetta had created the same stirrings in me in Beersheba— something similar must have been reaching thousands of Americans in those years after John Kennedy's election—but Bob had acted while most of the rest of us talked. And he took terrible risks. The three machine-gun bullets which had lodged in Jimmy Travis's neck were aimed at him....

One weekend late in the spring of 1965 Bob removed himself forever as a leader. At a SNCC conference in Atlanta he told the people who had worked with him the longest that he no longer wanted to be known as Bob Moses, and that he was determined to leave Mississippi, where he had struggled so long to build a movement. A cult of personality had developed around him, he said, and now it must vanish. People could be free only if they had no leaders, no idols.

He demolished an identity which thousands of people throughout America regarded as their source of moral authority. Bob Moses had become Bob Parris; he would never again head an organization but would work in some lonely corner of Alabama—and we were alone. I got very drunk the night I heard about his decision. He was lost to people like me, that was instantly clear; and I knew that I would feel his absence even more keenly than I felt the absence of John Kennedy. His act, however noble, seemed an admission that the hopes he had felt at the start of the decade, during those nights in New York when he listened to Odetta sing of her people and brooded on injustice in Mississippi, were unattainable in America. He had not stepped aside to make room for new leaders; the destruction of his identity seemed a naked admission that Bob Moses had failed. At least Kennedy was trying to bring change when he was murdered; Bob Moses, whose energy and dedication were much greater, was now asserting that no important changes could be inspired in America by people like himself. America had destroyed the politician who had sent our generation into action; now it was defeating the man who had supplied us with our courage and our vision.

The Making of an Un-American, 31, 64–65

 Have you had a hero-mentor whose work you have admired and whose life you have tried to emulate? What qualities did he or she possess that attracted you?

 Have you read about or seen a cult of hero-worship develop around a leader? Do you agree with Bob Moses that people can be free only if they have no leaders, no idols?

Have you experienced the loss of a leader? What were the consequences for you? For the agency, school, or social cause for whom the leader worked? Was the institution or movement demoralized? Can such discouragement be prevented?

 Are you perceived as a leader, mentor, or guardian spirit in the community in which you are serving? What will you do to prepare the way for your departure?

JAMES BOSWELL

After a tedious sail, which by our following various turnings of the coast of Mull, was extended to about forty miles, it gave us no small pleasure to perceive a light in the village at Icolmkill, in which almost all the inhabitants of the island live, close to where the ancient building stood. As we approached the shore, the tower of the cathedral, just discernible in the air, was a picturesque object.

When we had landed upon the sacred place, which, as long as I can remember, I had thought on with veneration, Dr. Johnson and I cordially embraced. We had long talked of visiting Icolmkill; and, from the lateness of the season, we were at times very doubtful whether we should be able to effect our purpose. To have seen it, even alone, would have given me great satisfaction; but the venerable scene was rendered much more pleasing by the company of my great and pious friend, who was no less affected by it than I was; and who has described the impressions it should make on the mind, with such strength of thought, and energy of language, that I shall quote his words, as conveying my own sensations much more forcibly than I am capable of doing:…

Early in the morning we surveyed the remains of antiquity at this place, accompanied by an illiterate fellow, as Cicerone, who called himself a descendant of a cousin of Saint Columba, the founder of the religious establishment here. As I knew that many persons had already examined them, and as I saw Dr. Johnson inspecting and measuring several of the ruins of which he has since given so full an account, my mind was quiescent; and I resolved to stroll among them at my ease, to take no trouble to investigate minutely, and only receive the general impression of solemn antiquity, and the particular ideas of such objects as should of themselves strike my attention.

A Journal of a Tour to the Hebrides with Samuel Johnson, 277–279

James Boswell so admired Samuel Johnson that he sometimes allowed Johnson to speak and think for him.

 Have you had a mentor upon whom you relied for ideas and words? Have you felt inadequate, believing that your mentor could "convey [your] own sensations much more forcibly than [you are] capable of doing?" Have you been tempted to "take no trouble to investigate minutely" yourself?

 What balance have you struck between welcoming the help and advice of another and taking responsibility yourself for your ideas and opinions?

STAGE IX

CELEBRATING
THE VICTORIES

The hero's journey is one of thresholds and gates, challenges and battles, and, if progress is made, one of victories large and small. Each mountain summited, flood forded, desert crossed, portal passed, mentor recognized, puzzle solved, and beast slain should be an occasion of rejoicing for the traveler. In even the most mundane of journeys, the traveler faces new situations whose mysteries he unshrouds.

Because not even a Hercules can endure unrelenting effort, everyone who travels the hero's path must pause for respite from time to time. These moments often coincide with the successful completion of a stage in the journey. The story of the hero is punctuated by celebrations of victories along the way with food, drink, dance, music, and entertainment. These events may even include the telling of a hero's tale! Provisions for the celebrations are often provided by a guardian spirit, who in some tales is unseen, as in the story of Beauty and the Beast and in the pilgrimmage of Saint Brendan. The merriment is usually followed by renewing sleep, coming when danger is passed and the victory won.

And, just as each journey has its successes to be celebrated, so also there are at least temporary failures. As we proceed along the hero's path, we continue to redefine the nature of the hero. When we wander in the wilderness, succumb to temptation, make a mistake, or fail to reach a goal, we need to be reminded that perfect heroes do not exist, and that if they did they would make trying companions and their stories would make for dull reading. All heroes take wrong turns from time to time; all encounter stumbling blocks. All have times of confusion about the direction they should take. Were it not so, there would be no challenges and therefore no victories.

Heroes of all time, real and imagined, have discovered that the most effective way of overcoming the obstacles is to accept defeat honestly. Humor is a primary weapon at points of failure. To own up to failure is itself a major victory, a milestone of accomplishment along the hero's path to adult responsibility. It is a way that human beings have managed in their journey through life to snatch victory from the jaws of defeat.

MARY KINGSLEY

I may remark on my own account that the Bubi villages do not often lie right on the path, but, like those you have to deal with up the Calabar, some little way off it. This is no doubt for the purpose of concealing their whereabouts from strangers, and it does it successfully too, for many a merry hour have I spent dodging up and down a path trying to make out at what particular point it was advisable to dive into the forest thicket to reach a village. But this cultivates habits of observation, and a short course of this work makes you recognise which tree is which along miles of a bush path as easily as you would shops in your own street at home.

Travels in West Africa, 60

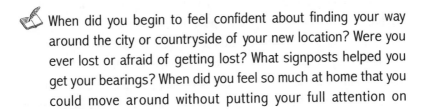 When did you begin to feel confident about finding your way around the city or countryside of your new location? Were you ever lost or afraid of getting lost? What signposts helped you get your bearings? When did you feel so much at home that you could move around without putting your full attention on directions?

One can think of the new geography as a metaphor for a new culture. Have you had experiences of feeling lost as you interact with people different from yourself? Describe an incident in which you realized that, at last, you were understanding your host culture and that they were understanding you. Have you reached the stage, if only briefly, where your host culture felt as familiar and as easily traversed as "shops in your own street at home?"

Have you paused to celebrate your achievement and share your success with friends?

EMILY BRONSON CONGER

It was a joy to get out of the native into the European parts of Shanghai and feel safe; and yet there was not a single thing, upon thinking it over, that one could say was alarming, not a disrespectful look from any one. I said upon reaching the outer gate, "Thank God, we are out of there alive and safe." It was the first experience only to be renewed with like scenes and impressions at Canton, with the same thankfulness of heart, too, for escape.

An Ohio Woman in the Philippines, 45

At first glance, this entry by Emily Conger may seem like a failure because she was so very anxious when not in the American and European parts of Shanghai and Canton (c. 1898). But her honesty and accuracy in admitting that she encountered nothing in the native section that could legitimately and objectively be a cause for alarm is surely a victory. Many tourists are never able to make distinctions between their own feelings and the external reality. Conger accepts her irrational feelings for what they are.

 Have you had feelings that you realized, at the time or later, had no basis in fact?

 Have you conquered your fears and plunged forward despite your unreasonable apprehension? Did you repeat the experience and was it easier the second and third times? Did you enjoy the sense of accomplishment?

SANA HASAN

We were divided into separate work teams, each with its own overseer. Some of us were to work in the fields, others on potato combines. Those aboard had to catch the potatoes, which the combines dug out of the soil at tremendous speed, wipe the mud and pebbles from them, and throw them into a huge bin. The other job—far more tiresome because of the bending involved—consisted of walking behind the potato combine and gathering the potatoes it had missed.

Our overseer assigned the combines to the females and the stoop work to the males. Because I disliked his patronizing assumption that women were suited only for lighter work, I traded places with one of the men, who was only too happy to oblige.

Hardly had the work begun, however, than I regretted my choice. My back ached, and my hands, raw from clawing into the rough soil, felt as if they were on fire. As the sun beat down upon me, I remembered a stout, red-faced Englishman I had seen in Upper Egypt who was felled by sunstroke. He lay stretched out on a bench in the garden of the Aswan Palace Hotel, alternately shrieking with pain and moaning in a mechanical, impersonal way. A black page boy in a flaming turban and ballooning pantaloons had run to fetch him ice, and he said as he attentively administered it, "You no worry, Meester Reechard, you be okay. Beoble no die from thees." But there wasn't a sliver of ice to be had here, not even a drop of cold water. Then I wondered what it was like to die of dehydration, and thought with pity of our poor soldiers who had been so thirsty in the Sinai desert during the '67 war that they had had to drink their urine.

After an hour's work, all sorts of mysterious objects began floating before my eyes, but I kept myself from fainting by conjuring up the embarrassing image of my body being carried off the field on a stretcher.

A jeep arrived with a water tank, and we drank at last. The overseer came by to ask me if I'd like to trade places with someone on the potato combine, now that it was halftime. Too proud to admit I was tired, I declined.

Those last hours were the worst. I had the feeling that this sweltering morning would never end; the rows of potatoes seemed interminable. I focused my envious eyes on the strong biceps of our handsome overseer; he seemed not in the least tired. How I hated the Israelis for their disgusting good health, and for all those yogurt-and-cucumber-salad breakfasts they had been fed since childhood!

Finally, the day was over. As I was dragging myself toward the big collection bin to throw in my last basket of potatoes, the overseer snatched it from me, yelling, "Not these, can't you see the ones on top are rotten?" He culled out some potatoes and, dropping them onto the ground, added, "Leave them, the Arabs will come for them. They always come around after we've finished a day's work to get what we've left behind. They'll eat anything."

Too tired to object, I let this remark pass. A minute later he came up to me and, patting me on the back, said that I should become a member of the kibbutz — implying that I had worked well. Swelling with pride, I looked patronizingly at the other women, who had done the easy job. Miriam Baratz, the first woman pioneer to earn the right to work in the fields alongside the men, back in 1910, could not have relished her hard-won recognition more than I did. I felt like dancing down the potato rows.

Enemy in the Promised Land, 93–94

Recalling your first days in your service assignment, when did you have your first sense of having been useful? Was it in doing what you expected or in doing something you had not anticipated was needed? Perhaps your help was simply in being yourself and being there. Was your contribution confirmed by others? In what ways?

 Have you willingly taken on a difficult assignment? Did you succeed? Was your success acknowledged by others? Was their recognition of your work approving or grudging?

 Have your victories in giving useful service changed your definition of yourself?

JAMES BOSWELL

One gentleman in company expressing his opinion "that *Fingal* was certainly genuine, for that he had heard a great part of it repeated in the original", Dr Johnson indignantly asked him, whether he understood the original; to which an answer being given in the negative, "Why then," said Dr Johnson, "we see to what this testimony comes: thus it is."

I mentioned this as a remarkable proof how liable the mind of man is to credulity, when not guarded by such strict examination as that which Dr Johnson habitually practised. The talents and integrity of the gentleman who made the remark, are unquestionable; yet, had not Dr Johnson made him advert to the consideration, that he who does not understand a language, cannot know that something which is recited to him is in that language, he might have believed, and reported to this hour, that he had "heard a great part of *Fingal* repeated in the original".

A Journal of a Tour to the Hebrides with Samuel Johnson, 310

The greatest intellectual challenge for the traveler-hero is discerning the truth of what she sees, hears and reads. Learning to question, to probe deeply, to go to the source of information and to weigh the intentions and motives of the speaker or writer is the task of the scholar and the mark of an educated person. Just as many students accept the reliability of anything in print, so many travelers accept without question information that comes through observation and conversation.

Reaching conclusions too quickly is a danger for those in a new situation. One often hears people who have but a brief encounter with a new culture speaking authoritatively, as if they were experts on that culture. (Those who know more are often too polite to correct them, but later, away from their hearing, ridicule them.) Victory for a traveler may lie more in suspending judgment than in being sure he understands.

 What truth have you uncovered? What was the process by which you arrived at your conclusion? Does it contradict widely accepted lore? Have you told others of your new knowledge? Has the combination of study with direct experience sharpened your skills of critical inquiry?

 About what have you suspended judgment? Are you gaining deeper perceptions each day about a complex issue facing the host society? If you have more questions now than you did in the beginning of the program, count yourself successful and pause to celebrate.

LANGSTON HUGHES

September approached and still I had made no headway with my father about going to college. He said Europe. I said New York. He said he wouldn't spend a penny to educate me in the United States. I asked him how long I had to stay in Mexico. He said until I decided to act wisely. Not caring what that meant, I made up my mind to see about getting away myself.

I had no money, but Tomas' father had asked me if I would teach his son English, so I accepted, receiving a modest fee. Probably because Tomas proved an apt pupil (and we pal'd around together quite a little, too), others heard of his rapid progress in speaking at English, and I soon found myself with more applicants for classes than I could accept. I raised my fee. When the schools opened, I was offered two positions as an English instructor — one in Señor Luis Tovar's business college, another in Señorita Padilla's private finishing school for girls. I was able to take them both, since Señorita Padilla's classes were in the mornings and Señior Tovar's in the afternoon and early evening.

I used the Berlitz method, all instruction entirely in English, and I found that it worked very well. My students really did learn something, and we had lots of fun together, besides. Very shortly, the mayor of the town sent for me and asked if I would give private lessons to his son and daughter at home.

The daughter was about sixteen and very beautiful, but the son was as bad a fifteen-year-old youngster as ever decided *not* to learn a word of anything. Result, neither girl nor boy got much beyond the words door and chair that winter, and I don't think they cared. They were rather spoiled, cream-colored children, who played tennis with a doctor's family, browner and more Indian-looking — one of the few Indian families considered "aristocracy" in Toluca, where Spanish blood still prevailed in the best circles and the exaltation of things Indian had not yet triumphed—for Diego Rivera was still in Paris.

As a teacher of English to the "best" families, I met a great many interesting people and my funds for escape grew apace. For the first time in my life, I had my own money to spend in decent amounts, to send my mother, and to save. All that winter I did not ask my father for a penny. And I knew by summer I would have enough to go to New York, so I began to plan my trip long before the winter was over. I dreamt about Harlem.

The Big Sea, 66–67

Langston Hughes found a way to his own independence, a way that was also of service to his students and to his mother. He also uncovered an interest and developed his skills in teaching.

 What interests have you uncovered, what skills developed?

He did not succeed with every student, but he realized that there were forces beyond his control and did not blame himself.

 What limitations have you experienced?

 Have you been able to own your victories and accept your defeats?

KATHLEEN NORRIS

The Plains are full of what a friend here calls "good telling stories," and while our sense of being forgotten by the rest of the world makes it all the more important that we preserve them and pass them on, instead we often neglect them. Perversely, we do not even claim those stories which have attracted national attention.... The young [are] disenfranchised while their elders drown in details, "story" reduced to the social column of the weekly newspaper that reports on family reunions, card parties, even shopping excursions to a neighboring town. But real story is as hardy as grass, and it survives in Dakota in oral form. Good storytelling is one thing rural whites and Indians have in common. But Native Americans have learned through harsh necessity that people who survive encroachment by another culture need story to survive. And a storytelling tradition is something Plains people share with both ancient and contemporary monks: we learn our ways of being and reinforce our values by telling tales about each other.

Dakota: A Spiritual Geography, 5–6

Telling the story of a people is essential to sustaining the culture, and often represents a victory even in the midst of oppression or neglect.

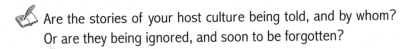 Are the stories of your host culture being told, and by whom? Or are they being ignored, and soon to be forgotten?

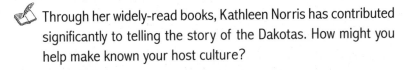 Through her widely-read books, Kathleen Norris has contributed significantly to telling the story of the Dakotas. How might you help make known your host culture?

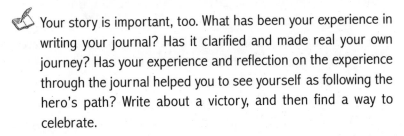 Your story is important, too. What has been your experience in writing your journal? Has it clarified and made real your own journey? Has your experience and reflection on the experience through the journal helped you to see yourself as following the hero's path? Write about a victory, and then find a way to celebrate.

PAUL COWAN

From the day I met Nick he made me feel somewhat guilty. As we discussed our reactions to the draft, very early in the training session, I discovered, as I frequently would in Guayaquil, that he was often able to act at times when I preferred to cling to the safety of continued discussions. Though he had joined the Peace Corps to stay out of the army, too, he had been defying his local board throughout the previous fall — the period when I decided to publish an objective article about General Hershey in the *Voice* instead of using that interview as an opening into a more risky exploration of my own tangled objections to the draft and the war. When Nick had been ordered to take his preinduction physical in San Francisco he refused to sign the oath asserting that he had never belonged to any of the organizations on the Attorney General's list. "They had no right to ask me a question like that," he said. For several months thereafter the FBI pursued him, both by letter and through interviews with his friends. Whenever he received a correspondence from them he underlined it, wrote sarcastic comments in the margins, and sent it back without complying with any particular request. Finally, the FBI asked him whether he had worked with Communists. He answered frankly that he didn't know. "What I believe in doing I do, without asking who my allies are."

But Nick didn't confuse particular beliefs with ideological certainties. He felt somewhat uncomfortable in the peace movement because many of the radicals he met there seemed as unquestioningly committed to unexamined points of view as his neighbors had been in Riverside, California. Their intolerance often offended him.

Nick and Ed have earned the ideas that many members of the intellectual class inherit.

I was never forced to brawl with my family over fundamental assumptions. We fight, of course, but usually over issues

216

that are more stylistic than substantial. My parents object when I dress sloppily or use four-letter words in print or insist on expressing my ideas so angrily that I insult their friends and can't function inside ... Ed and Nick are force[d] to quarrel with their families over substantive issues. Their disagreements with their parents and many of the schoolmates they have known for fifteen or twenty years are fundamental, but they continue to love the people who reject their new beliefs. In order to express their loyalty, to protect shared emotions which they cherish, they have evolved a style which is much gentler than mine. They converse with people I dismiss, seek reconciliation where I am tempted to rupture a relationship. The man I mock as a Babbitt Nick perceives as the friendly Shriner who used to live next door to him in California, his Dad's good friend who took him hunting on dozens of happy Sunday mornings. I tend to denounce his ideas a little testily; Nick will spend hours talking with him, human to human, exchange personal reminiscences, gently force him to question assumptions he has never before considered.

The Making of an Un-American, 123–124

Paul Cowan identifies qualities he admires in his friends Ed and Nick. He sees as victories Nick's commitment to action, his questioning of ideology which others took up without examination, and the ability of both Nick and Ed to maintain friendships with those with whom they strongly disagreed.

 Have you seen qualities in others that you admire, qualities that if you were to acquire you would count among your victories?

 Have you made a friend in your new community or among your fellow students of someone with whom you are able to disagree on many important issues? Has this been a victory for you? For him?

Charting a Hero's Journey

OCTAVIO PAZ

British influence would have been limited to a very few had it not been for the introduction of the English system of education. This decision was made in 1835 under the recommendation of Lord Macaulay, then a man of thirty-four, who the year before had been named president of the Commission of Public Instruction. One should add that twelve years earlier, in a letter to the Governor General, Ram Mohan Roy, now known as the "father of modern India," had requested that schools be established in Bengal to teach the natives English rather than Persian or Sanskrit: "I beg your Lordship will be pleased to compare the state of Science and Literature in Europe before the time of Lord Bacon with the progress in knowledge made since he wrote .... [To adopt] the Sanskrit system of education ... would be best calculated to keep this country in darkness." Roy admired Hindu tradition and never converted to Christianity; his argument cannot be seen as a betrayal. As for Macaulay, he based his decision both on his evident disdain for Hindu and Muslim tradition and on his exalted view of European culture, particularly the English language. He saw English, not unreasonably, as the universal language of the future. Macaulay's contempt for Asian cultures was due to his ignorance of their traditions, a rare error of perspective for a historian of his distinction. Nevertheless, he was essentially right: since the thirteenth century, neither the Hindus nor the Muslims had produced a body of knowledge or of literary and artistic works comparable to that of the Europeans. The two civilizations were petrified spiritually, and in perpetual political and social turmoil.

Macaulay's plan was to open the world of modern culture to the Indians, and in his defense he cited the precedent of Russia: "Within the last hundred and twenty years, a nation, which has previously been in a state as barbarous as that in which our ancestors were before the Crusades, has gradually emerged from the ignorance in which it was sunk, and has taken its place among civilized communities.... The languages of western Europe civilized Russia. I cannot doubt that they will do for the Hindoo what they have done for the Tartar." Macaulay admitted that it was impossible to extend the British system of education to the entire population. This is another difference from Spanish rule in the Americas: the imposition of the Spanish language on the indigenous population had two goals, one political-administrative and the other religious. Neither goal was intended by Macaulay or the British administration. Macaulay, in fact, stated, "It is impossible for us, with our limited means, to attempt to educate the body of the people. We must at present do our best to form a class who may be interpreters between us and the millions whom we govern; a class of persons, Indian in blood and color, but English in tastes, opinions, morals, and in intellect." This class, he added, would gradually extend modern knowledge to the great mass of the population.

Macaulay's proposal was a success.

In Light of India, 103–105

The hero's journey is an individual story, but also may be told of a people. In a nation's history there are victories which bring good while displacing older systems.

 Who brought the system of education to your host country? What did it bring that was positive and what negative? What did it displace that had been positive, what negative, and for whom?

 What do you think about the "victory" of the English language as the universal language of the modern world? What is made possible by this recent development? What is lost?

 Octavio Paz concludes that Macaulay's proposal was a success. Applying Macaulay's principles to your host nation, describe a change that you have studied in history or sociology that you evaluate as a success.

Anthony Winkler

We plodded on. Five days a week. Two hours every evening. Through Shakespeare and Shaw and Swift and Donne and Chaucer. We read and analyzed and studied and made notes. I lectured and explicated the text and tried to give them a flavour for the kind of academic exegesis they would be expected to write. We pored over the ruminations of critics, forewords by famous scholars, afterwords by the authors and their contemporaries, footnotes by interpreters, endnotes by anthologizers and compilers. Many a night it took all my self-control not to hurl the books against a wall and scream, "Piss on Swift and Donne and Dryden, piss on the whole lot of them!" We plodded on. Day in and day out. Moonlight, humidity and thunderstorm. Croaking lizards and whistling frogs and whining mosquitoes. We met in the same empty classroom, sat in the same chairs, faced the same scribbled-over blackboard, and read the same authors over and over and over.

Then, with the sneakiness of a glacier, our time had suddenly come. The exam was tomorrow.

My A level students and I had had our final meeting, had closed the books once and for all, and had spent our last study hour or two congratulating ourselves on work well done. Since the girls did not have the entrance fees for the exam, I had scraped together the hundred dollars and lent it to them. The A level exams would be held in Kingston and would coincide with the week of island-wide qualifying exams administered to all graduating teachers by the Ministry. There was to be much frenzied shuttling back and forth from Kingston to Longstreet, and the girls were going to be in for a gruelling week of sitting for both the Ministry's and the A level exams. But as we wandered out of the classroom that last night, the dormitory buildings blazing with the lights of last-minute crammers and a cool mountain breeze fanning us with the blossoms of the flowering poui trees, we felt as lighthearted and giddy as underground miners getting a first glimpse of the clear night sky after a long shift.

"The exam tree blooming," Mavis said, sniffing the air with pleasure.

"Yes," Jeanie said softly. "When the poui blossom, exam time come."

And the pouis were blossoming in all their fleeting and triumphant glory during these soft days, carpeting the earth with fallen petals.

Another generation of Jamaican children were being summoned to the bar.

Dr. Levy called me into his office early in the morning. He had lately moved his administrative throne to a remote rear room on the second floor of a concrete annex recently added on to the old wooden administration building. You walked up the stairs and entered a tremendous anteroom so austerely empty of furniture that your footsteps echoed as if in a fog, and it was guarded by a trio of two glum typists and the doctor's secretary. Three small desks with battered manual typewriters were moored in an ocean of pastel tile, and the tang of barely cured concrete and freshly applied whitewash immediately tickled your nose. The typists generally had little or nothing to type, and the secretary, who had no phone to answer, spent most of her time reading magazines or sticking her head out the window to scold the boisterous labourers below whose profanity occasionally drifted in and buzzed her ears. Because of ill-fitting dentures that stretched her lips and gave her an ugly overbite, she wore the grimace of a seasoned battle-axe and seemed sour and bad-tempered, but, in truth, she was a soft-spoken and sweet-natured woman whose only quirk was a Christian aversion to blasphemy and bad words. I had scarcely settled in the straight-backed chair before his desk when the doctor, looking officious and abnormally solemn, broke the news. The girls would not be allowed to sit for the A level exams.

At first I thought I had heard him wrong, so I asked him please to repeat what he had just said.

The girls would not be allowed to sit for the A level exams, he said again, this time with a flinty grimness. The A level exam conflicted with the Ministry's island-wide exam.

"But you knew that last year, sah. You knew that six months ago. I asked you about that before I agreed to tutor them."

Nevertheless, they would not be allowed to sit because of the conflict in the scheduling.

"Conflict? What rass conflict? You knew about the rass conflict ten months ago!"

I do not know how he did it, but right before my eyes he increased in volume and girth and cubic capacity until he had swelled into a mountainous presence of offended dignity.

"You dare use that word to me?"

"Rass? You think dat word is all I going use? I teach dese two students for a whole rass year with your permission, and now you tell me dat dey can't take de exam?"

"You have the nerve to address me in that tone, sir!"

I used other words, too. I was in such a blind and uncontrollable rage that I could hardly talk. I cursed and swore until the profanities seemed to lacerate my lips as they spewed out my mouth. Then I stormed out of the room, leaving him sputtering.

"Him is a dirty rass!" I roared at the head of the stairs, the obscenity caroming off the freshly laid walls as if bellowed in a grotto.

This was not America. Here rass mattered.

Here rass was virulent and cathartic.

"Lawd God, Missah Winkler" the doctor's secretary cried in horror, her hand flying to her mouth. "Lawd God, sah!"

I stomped downstairs and broke the news to my two students, who were dressed and waiting with their pencils and pens and exercise books to journey to the examiner's office in Kingston. Jeanie stared out the window and shrugged with heavy resignation. Mavis narrowed her eyes, leaned forward and spat evilly at me,

"Don't I tell you, Missah Winkler? You remember when I tell you dat, sah? You don't remember, sah?"

"I remember," I mumbled. "I can't believe he did this to us. I can't believe it."

"I believe it, yes!" she crowed with boundless malice and vindication. "Is so a Jamaica man do him own people. I tell you dat already! You don't remember?"

"I remember," I capitulated abjectly. "I remember."

Going Home to Teach, 257–260

Sometimes in service, and for a variety of reasons, defeat is snatched from the very jaws of victory. Winkler gives us a picture of his fury at learning that his year of tutoring had been a waste for him and for his students.

 Are there any victories to be claimed here? Anthony Winkler left Jamaica the next week. What would you have done? Was the expression of his anger a victory or a sign of his defeat?

One of the two students Winkler tutored gave up her education, but the other, after thirteen years of hard work and saving, went to university and eventually to law school.

 Have you had an experience in service in which you felt close to a victory, only to have your hopes dashed? How common is the experience for the people with whom you are working and serving? How do they cope? Do you consider their ways of coping a victory or a defeat for them? How do they consider your means of coping with disappointment?

Stage X

Discovering
the Boon

A long the road there comes the time when the hero realizes
that she has been not only on an adventure but on a quest.
The climax comes when she finds the object of her search. The
scales drop from her eyes and she sees the world and herself in
new, life-giving, and life-transforming ways.

Called in classic literature "the boon," the good that the
hero was seeking is discovered or recovered in an instant of
blinding light. Fire is captured, the Holy Grail recovered, the
Cosmos experienced, the Great Idea realized, the Prime Mover
known, the Meaning of Life revealed.

But often, in real life, the boon steals in, showing its face in
the quiet moments of retreat and reflection. And it generally
comes from a series of thoughts and events. These collective
experiences finally add up to something important—a new
understanding of life and its meaning, a new set of skills, an
appreciation of one's talents and limitations, and particularly
the purpose and meaning of the life of the adventurer-sojourner-
pilgrim-hero.

The boon is often seen as a gift, coming from a source more
powerful than the hero himself. But whatever the source, the
"lifetransmuting trophy" requires that the hero "now begin
the labor of bringing the runes of wisdom, the Golden Fleece,
the sleeping princess, back into the kingdom of humanity, where
the boon may redound to the renewing of the community,

nation, the planet or ten thousand worlds." [11] A good discovered but not returned leaves the hero's destiny forever in suspension, and the journey but half finished.

Having found the object of the search, the hero is left with the two stages of the journey that sages call the most difficult of all. But be comforted. For the hero commissioned "to return to the world with some elixir for the restoration of society, the final stages [are] supported by all the powers of the supernatural." [12]

The hero prepares for the return, to bring home the discovered good for the benefit of others. Societies see such returning heroes as the bearers of fresh energy and new ideas, and as the day-spring that comes afresh with each generation, necessary to sustain and renew life.

KATHLEEN NORRIS

The farmers I know in Dakota … live in what they laconically refer to as "next-year country."

We hold on to hopes for next year every year in western Dakota: hoping that droughts will end; hoping that our crops won't be hailed out in the few rainstorms that come; hoping that it won't be too windy on the day we harvest, blowing away five bushels an acre; hoping (usually against hope) that if we get a fair crop, we'll be able to get a fair price for it. Sometimes survival is the only blessing that the terrifying angel of the Plains bestows.

Dakota: A Spiritual Geography, 7

Hope has been named as one of the great boons of human life. No matter how bad a situation may appear, if hope remains all is not lost.

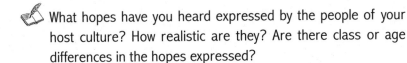 What hopes have you heard expressed by the people of your host culture? How realistic are they? Are there class or age differences in the hopes expressed?

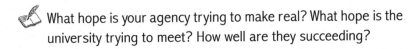 What hope is your agency trying to make real? What hope is the university trying to meet? How well are they succeeding?

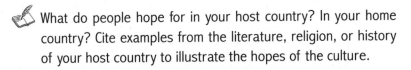 What do people hope for in your host country? In your home country? Cite examples from the literature, religion, or history of your host country to illustrate the hopes of the culture.

Percy Bysshe Shelley wrote these lines in his poem *Prometheus Unbound:*

> ...to hope, till Hope creates
> ...the thing it contemplates.[13]

 What does he mean? Do you believe this is ever true? Can you give an example?

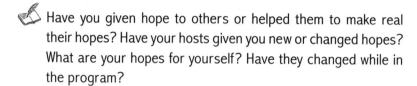 Have you given hope to others or helped them to make real their hopes? Have your hosts given you new or changed hopes? What are your hopes for yourself? Have they changed while in the program?

PAUL COWAN

We had been in the Peace Corps for only nine months, in Guayaquil for six, but I already felt as if I had dropped off the plane of reality that contained Harvard, New York, and the movement, off and into Nixonia.

Instead of worrying where my next article would be published, or how the next antiwar demonstration would be orchestrated, or debating whether Tom Hayden and Staughton Lynd should have gone to Bobby Kennedy's apartment to talk about the war in Vietnam, we had been trying to push our way past the Peace Corps' definition of our role in the barrios and maneuver ourselves into working relations with Ecuadorians who seemed relatively progressive. Rachel and I had grown much closer to each other in the process and learned a frightening amount about America. In many ways, the battles we were fighting seemed to us much more important than the battles people waged in the sectarian left and at the Big Fiesta. Nevertheless, we bad been arguing with Peace Corps people for so long that we had begun to accept their terms, their definitions of flexibility, of democracy, of reasonable dissent. We could see past Erich Hofmann but no longer as far as Bob Moses. I could insist to Caleb Roehrig that the Peace Corps' marriage rule was a form of *apartheid,* but I could not quite believe my own memory when it said that Rachel and I had once belonged to a group of people who had risked their lives to combat that sort of thing in Mississippi.

Then we went to Mexico City to spend Christmas with Rachel's family and my brother....

We talked to our families almost incessantly, but we relaxed, too. Certainly we were lucky to be in Mexico City...to walk through its festive parks, to eat its rich foods, to explore its fascinating ruins. But we would have laughed together and loved each other wherever we had been. For the first time since training began, Rachel and I were completely free of the

229

definitions which the Peace Corps had imposed on our personalities. We didn't fear that our integrity depended on our willingness to fight the bigotry of our peers, and that feeling persuaded us at last that we were not fanatics or outcasts or fools but ordinary human beings, born into a crippled time, who were honestly seeking a way to do nothing more complex than build a productive, loving life for ourselves and our friends.

The Making of an Un-American, 287–289

For the young and intense Paul Cowan, who incessantly fought with the institutions and cultures within which he was working, the boon came in two ways: by the relationship with his beloved new wife and by getting away from the place where he was serving and where he had allowed the burden of the world to rest on his shoulders. Within the intimacy of his marriage and on vacation in a land where he was to be but briefly and for which he could assume no responsibility, he found a peace that had previously eluded him.

 How might you imagine his relationships and understanding were changed as a result of his experience with Rachel in Mexico?

 Have you found a boon in any friendship or in getting away from heavy demands and expectations? Have you learned any lessons from these experiences that will shape your decisions and manner of life in the future?

We can readily imagine the ways in which accepting responsibility becomes a boon to others. But are there ways in which laying aside overwhelming feelings of responsibility becomes a boon for others?

 Are there famous friendships in the culture of your host nation that are seen not only as boons to the friends, but as boons to the nation? What close relationship have you seen in your host family, in the agency where you are serving or at the university that are boons to a wider world? Who benefits from this friendship, and in what ways?

LANGSTON HUGHES

At the annual festival bullfight for the charities of la Cavadonga, when the belles of Mexico City, in their lace mantillas, drove about the arena in open carriages preceding the fight, and the National Band played, and the *Presidente de la Republica* was there, and Sanchez Mejias made the hair stand on your head and cold chills run down your back with the daring and beauty of his *veronicas,* after the fight there was a great rush into the ring on the part of many of the young men in the crowd, to lift the famous fighters on their shoulders or to carry off a pair of golden banderillas as a souvenir, with the warm blood still on them. I dived for the ring, too, the moment the fight was over. In leaping the *barrera*, I tore my only good trousers from knee to ankle — but I got my banderillas.

After the fights, I would usually have supper with the three charming and aging Mexican sisters, the Patiños, friends of my father's, who lived near the Zocalo, just back of the cathedral, and who always invited me to vespers. To please them, I would go to vespers, and I began to love the great, dusky, candle-lighted interiors of the vast Mexican churches, smoky with incense and filled with sad virgins and gruesome crucifixes with real thorns on the Christ-head, and what seemed to be real blood gushing forth from His side, thick and red as the blood of the bulls I had seen killed in the afternoon. In the evenings I might go to see Margarita Xirgu, or Virginia Fabregas in some bad Spanish play, over-acted and sticky like the cakes in our Toluca sweet shop.

Meanwhile, ambitiously, I began to try to write prose. I tried to write about a bullfight, but could never capture it on paper. Bullfights are very hard things to put down on paper — like trying to describe the ballet.

Almost every week-end that winter, now that I was earning my own money, I went to the bullfights in Mexico City. Rudolfo

Gaona was the famous Mexican matador of the day, a stocky Indian of great art and bravery. Sanchez Mejias was there from Spain that season, greatly acclaimed, as well as Juan Silveti, and a younger fighter called Juan Luis de la Rosa, who did not win much favor with the crowd. One afternoon, in the sunset, at the end of a six-bull corrida, (bulls from the Duque de Veragua) I saw de la Rosa trying to kill his final bull amidst a shower of cushions, canes, paper bags, and anything else throwable that an irate crowd could hurl at him. But he stuck it out, and finally the enormous animal slid to his knees, bleeding on the sand. But the matador was soundly hissed as he left the ring.

The Big Sea, 69–70

Poetry had come easily and at a tender age to Langston Hughes, but he had been unable to write prose. The stimuli of the bullfight and of the church—two things he resisted—seemed to free him to write prose although the subject of his prose was neither bullfighting nor religion.

 Have you been freed in any way to think or do something that has previously eluded you? To what do you attribute this liberation? A boon to you, is it also something you will be able to return for the good of others?

SAMUEL JOHNSON

There is one subject of philosophical curiosity to be found in Edinburgh, which no other city has to show; a college of the deaf and dumb, who are taught to speak, to read, to write, and to practise arithmetic, by a gentleman whose name is Braidwood. The number which attends him is, I think, about twelve, which he brings together into a little school, and instructs according to their several degrees of proficiency.

I do not mean to mention the instruction of the deaf as new. Having been first practised upon the son of a Constable of Spain, it was afterwards cultivated with much emulation in England, by Wallis and Holder, and was lately professed by Mr. Baker, who once flattered me with hopes of seeing his method published. How far any former teachers have succeeded, it is not easy to know; the improvement of Mr. Braidwood's pupils is wonderful. They not only speak, write, and understand what is written, but if he that speaks looks towards them, and modifies his organs by distinct and full utterance, they know so well what is spoken, that it is an expression scarcely figurative to say, they hear with the eye. That any have attained to the power, mentioned by Burnet, of feeling sounds, by laying a hand on the speaker's mouth, I know not; but I have seen so much, that I can believe more; a single word, or a short sentence, I think, may possibly be so distinguished.

It will readily be supposed by those that consider this subject, that Mr. Braidwood's scholars spell accurately. Orthography is vitiated among such as learn first to speak and then to write, by imperfect notions of the relation between letters and vocal utterance; but to those students every character is of equal importance; for letters are to them not symbols of names, but of things; when they write they do not represent a sound, but delineate a form.

This school I visited, and found some of the scholars waiting for their master, whom they are said to receive at his entrance with smiling countenances and sparkling eyes, delighted with the hope of new ideas. One of the young ladies had her slate before her, on which I wrote a question consisting of three figures, to be multiplied by two figures. She looked upon it, and quivering her fingers in a manner which I thought very pretty, but of which I know not whether it was art or play, multiplied the sum regularly in two lines, observing the decimal place; but did not add the two lines together, probably disdaining so easy an operation. I pointed at the place where the sum total should stand, and she noted it with such expedition as seemed to show that she had it only to write.

It was pleasing to see one of the most desperate of human calamities capable of so much help; whatever enlarges hope will exalt courage; after having seen the deaf taught arithmetic, Who would be afraid to cultivate the Hebrides?

A Journey to the Western Islands of Scotland, 238–240

That Samuel Johnson, whose life was a study in elegance of language and manners, should pronounce Scotland worthy on the basis of a school for the deaf is a tribute both to the teacher, Mr. Braidwood, and to himself. What a change from Johnson's pre-journey attitudes that included the packing of pistols for his journey and declaring the country he was to visit uncivilized!

 What good have you discovered as a way of judging your host culture? Are there "Mr. Braidwood"s among your hosts whom you have come to admire and whose story you will share with others when you return home? How will this enlarge your hearers' understanding of the place you have been?

 What do you think of Johnson's idea that the right way to judge a culture lies in its treatment of the less fortunate?

Emily Bronson Conger

The field corn which I saw was of such an inferior grade that it never occurred to me to try it; indeed, they do not bring it to market until it is out of the milk.

On my return home I planted a few kernels as an experiment. There never was a more insignificant looking stalk of corn in our garden. With misgivings we made trial of the scrubby looking ears. To our surprise it was the best we ever had on our table. It seemed too good to be true. I gave several messes to my friends and this year am hoping to give pleasure to many others. I denied myself the delicious product that many might have seed for this spring....

I had a small brass dagger which I used to carry for defense and, upon showing it to some of my friends, since my return, I was asked if I saw this dagger made, because if I knew the secret of its annealing it would be worth a fortune to me....I had missed a golden chance for I had often visited a rude foundry where they made bolos and other articles, but it did not occur to me that there could be anything of value to expert workmen at home in these crude hand processes.

An Ohio Woman in the Philippines, 100–102

It is no surprise that Emily Conger thought to bring home seeds. All American families who moved west carried seeds with them. She was but following the Ohio family wisdom.

 What will you bring home — ideas, objects, values — that complement the traditions of home?

 Conger admits that although she was a careful observer, she nonetheless missed opportunities. What might you have missed by way of discovering a boon? Have there been opportunities in your study abroad or community service which you bypassed, now to your regret?

OCTAVIO PAZ

Of course, it is impossible to foresee the future turn of events. In politics and history, perhaps in everything, that unknown power the ancients called Fate is always at work. Without forgetting this, I must add that, in politics as well as in private life, the surest method for resolving conflicts, however slowly, is dialogue. Talking with our adversary, we become our own interlocutor. This is the essence of democracy. Its preservation entails the conservation of the project of the founders of modern India: a state that encompasses diversity without suppressing it. It is a task that demands realism and imagination, and, at the same time, a certain virtue. There is a terrible law: all great historical creation has been built upon sacrifice. In the case of Indian democracy, the blood of a just man, Mahatma Gandhi, and also that of Indira, her son Rajiv, and countless innocent victims. All of them died so that one day Hindus, Muslims, Sikhs, and the others could talk in peace.

In Light of India, 132–133

Octavio Paz raises several possible boons—religion, secularism, democracy, dialogue.

 What do you see as possible boons for addressing the evils of the world?

 What does he mean when he says "Talking with our adversary, we become our own interlocutor?" Are there examples in the history of your host nation or community in which the questions posed by intercultural contact stimulated self-questioning that eventually caused a change in policy or customs?

 Describe an experience in which, by talking with an adversary, you became your own interlocutor.

 Paz says that sacrifice is the foundation of all great historical creation. Do you agree? What sacrifice will be needed by your host society if the social problems you have encountered are to be creatively and successfully addressed?

 What sacrifices do you believe you are called upon to make?

SANA HASAN

When she got to the kibbutz, she found that someone had already broken the news to her mother-in-law, who had just turned eighty and had to bear the loss of her husband, her son, and now her grandson. A strongly built, square-jawed Slav of sturdy pioneering stock, Sara Belahofsky was a very dignified woman and, as usual, displayed nothing of her grief. She continued to rise punctually at seven every morning, but the work that had always been such a joy she now went about mechanically. Even the garden in which she had taken such pride no longer meant anything to her. Something had broken. Her one consolation was her other grandson, Shoshana's son, Roni. Shoshana told me, "After David was killed, Mother used to say to me, 'You will see, by the time Roni gets to the Sinai there will be peace, I am sure of it.' "

A few years later, it was Shoshana's turn to take the trip abroad....

She was in London when the telephone rang at midnight. Roni had been killed. He had fallen along the Suez Canal on the first day of the 1973 war, when the Egyptian troops stormed the Bar-Lev line. He was nineteen. Shoshana flew back immediately.

Shoshana had no time to cry for her son because she had to pull herself together and take care of her mother. She had dreaded breaking the news of Roni's death to his grandmother, and indeed Roni's loss was more than Sara Belahofsky could endure. Little by little, everything became confused for her. She would suddenly get up and say to Shoshana, "We have to go to Roni's ... to David's ... to Joseph's funeral." "You know, David has come back, he's not dead."

"It's a horrible thing to say," Shoshana said, "but I suffered so much seeing her that way that I used to wish her dead. But when she died, it was terrible. Everything came together—her death, the death of Father, of Joseph, of David and Roni. I couldn't take it anymore, I collapsed. Then I looked around me; I saw others in the kibbutz who had also just lost sons in the war, and I realized that I had to shake myself out of my depression and help them. I remembered Mother's dying words. She was in the hospital and suddenly she got up. A friend asked her, 'Where are you going, Sara?' and she answered, 'I'm going on duty, I have to guard.' And the friend said to her, 'Sleep, Sara. Don't worry. Shoshana will take over from you.' "

On hearing this, I grasped for the first time the significance of the five huge basalt tombstones in the kibbutz cemetery: they symbolized the strength of the Belahofsky clan, their fortitude in the face of overpowering sacrifice. Who could help admiring them? There was something majestic about their pain. And yet those tombstones also symbolized a fortress the Belahofskys had passed on to their children to enable them to fight war after war without question. It was this aspect of their impossible heroism I found difficult to accept. How could all they had gone through not have altered their trust in their leaders, their unwearied devotion to their country? While I was moved by their pain, sometimes, in noting the admiring glances cast upon them in the dining room, I struggled in vain to banish from my mind the suspicion that they savored their martyrdom. There seemed to be a secret obstinacy in that sorrow, something I could not understand — as if their grief were a form of strength that packed the force of a weapon. Could their sorrow be hostile? Before its incomprehensibility I became conscious of anger, my old anger against Israel reawakened. Were they not exploiting their grief the way Israel sometimes did the Holocaust victims and its own war dead — for political ends? And if so, was it not incumbent on me to resist being manipulated? My heart constantly vacillated between deep sympathy and mistrust. I felt I could not pity them without a risk.

I became haunted by the price this family had paid for the state of Israel, and wondered whether they ever felt that it was too high. One day when I was in Shoshana's house, I inquired,

"Did you ever ask yourself if the demand for Isaac's sacrifice was justified?"

She looked at me uncomprehendingly. It was clear she was reluctant to answer. But at that moment I was driven by such savage curiosity that I would have scratched her heart out to get at the truth. I asked her bluntly, "Did you ever think that if your leaders had been more flexible, your son might still be alive today?"

She began to tremble, and finally she answered: "I could wonder whether my son would still be alive if our government had been more conciliatory, and I could wonder about many other sophisticated things. There are so many questions you can raise.... "

She was very agitated, but I went on with heartless obstinacy to spell out all the opportunities for peace that had been lost because of Israel's intransigence. I subjected her to a scathing account of all the wars, leading up to the 1973 war, that could have been avoided had it not been for Golda Meir's policy of creeping annexation—her bad faith in claiming that everything was negotiable if only the Arabs would come to the bargaining table without conditions, even as new Jewish settlements kept being established in the occupied territories.

She listened to me with a look of complete bewilderment on her face and then stammered: "I—I—I don't know... Maybe you're right, but it's best not to think too much about... You see, when there is a war, you have no choice. You have to say, 'My country needs soldiers, so *here I am to do it.' "*

A flood of tears ended her words.

Terrified by the spectacle of this sorrow I was beginning to comprehend, and ashamed of having provoked it, I wanted to flee. Instead, I tried to console her. I apologized and begged her not to cry, but all to no avail.

As I stood helpless and numb before the frenzy of her grief, Shoshana looked up at me kindly and said, "Don't worry, it does me good, I haven't cried since Mother died."

When I left her that evening, I tried to quiet my guilty conscience by telling myself that what I had done was justified by the need to make people less ready in the future to serve up their children as cannon fodder for the wars brought on by the ambitious designs of their leaders. But I realized, of course, that like the generation of the founders before her, Shoshana was strong in her innocent patriotism and courageous in her single-minded devotion, and I had no right to rob her of this. By tormenting her, I had been trying to escape my own uneasiness. Every time she mourned her son, I would travel back to those gatherings in Harvard's Middle East Center reading room, when my Arab friends and I would gleefully pore over the newspapers, counting casualty figures and drawing up inventories of all the tanks "we" were blowing up during the 1973 war on the Bar-Lev line. It was almost impossible to believe that all this had happened only a few months before, impossible to contemplate that one of the casualties "they" suffered had been Shoshana's son. Here, among the people who paid for the politicians' wars, it was impossible to remove myself from their agony.

Enemy in the Promised Land, 110–113

In what was for her enemy territory, Sana Hasan learned to feel compassion and even empathy. She came to understand the complexity of human situations and to forgo the simple designations of "we" and "they." She experienced profoundly the implications for individual lives of choices made and actions taken by national leaders. In the face of it all, she continued to ask hard questions.

 Describe a moment in which you felt compassion or empathy for one you previously had dismissed or despised. Or, describe an incident in which you realized complexity.

 What hard questions do you believe should be asked of your host culture?

 What are the rights and wrongs of Hasan's pushing her troubling questions on the grieving woman?

 How will the understanding you have achieved through your experience and reflection be turned into a boon for others?

Mary Kingsley

The difficulty of the language is, however, far less than the whole set of difficulties with your own mind. Unless you can make it pliant enough to follow the African idea step by step, however much care you may take, you will not bag your game. I heard an account the other day — I have forgotten where — of a representative of her Majesty in Africa who went out for a day's antelope shooting. There were plenty of antelope about, and he stalked them with great care; but always, just before he got within shot of the game, they saw something and bolted. Knowing he and the boy behind him had been making no sound and could not have been seen, he stalked on, but always with the same result; until happening to look round, he saw the boy behind him was supporting the dignity of the Empire at large, and this representative of it in particular, by steadfastly holding aloft the consular flag. Well, if you go hunting the African idea with the flag of your own religion or opinions floating ostentatiously over you, you will similarly get a very poor bag.

A few hints as to your mental outfit when starting on this port may be useful. Before starting for West Africa, burn all your notions about sun-myths and worship of the elemental forces. My own opinion is you had better also burn the notion, although it is fashionable, that human beings got their first notion of the origin of the soul from dreams.

I went out with my mind full of the deductions of every book on Ethnology, German or English, that I had read during fifteen years — and being a good Cambridge person, I was particularly confident that from Mr. Frazer's book, *The Golden Bough,* I had got a semi-universal key to the underlying idea of native custom and belief. But I soon found this was very far from being the case. His idea is a true key to a certain quantity of facts, but in West Africa only to a limited quantity.

I do not say, do not read Ethnology — by all means do so; and above all things read, until you know it by heart, *Primitive*

244

Culture, by Dr. E. B. Tylor, regarding which book I may say that I have never found a fact that flew in the face of the carefully made, broad-minded deductions of this greatest of Ethnologists. In addition you must know your Westermarck on *Human Marriage,* and your Waitz *Anthropologie,* and your Topinard— not that you need expect to go measuring people's skulls and chests as this last named authority expects you to do, for no self-respecting person black or white likes that sort of thing from the hands of an utter stranger, and if you attempt it you'll get yourself disliked in West Africa. Add to this the knowledge of all A. B. Ellis's works; Burton's *Anatomy of Melancholy;* Pliny's *Natural History;* and as much of Aristotle as possible. If you have a good knowledge of the Greek and Latin classics, I think it would be an immense advantage; an advantage I do not possess, for my classical knowledge is scrappy, and in place of it I have a knowledge of Red Indian dogma: a dogma by the way that seems to me much nearer the African in type than Asiatic forms of dogma.

Armed with these instruments of observation, with a little industry and care you should in the mill of your mind be able to make the varied tangled rag-bag of facts that you will soon become possessed of into a paper....

I give this as a sample of African stories. It is far more connected and keeps to the point in a far more businesslike way than most of them. They are of great interest when you know the locality and the tribe they come from; but I am sure if you were to bring home a heap of stories like this, and empty them over any distinguished ethnologist's head, without ticketing them with the culture of the tribe they belonged to, the conditions it lives under, and so forth, you would stun him with the seeming inter-contradiction of some, and utter pointlessness of the rest, and he would give up ethnology and hurriedly devote his remaining years to the attempt to collect a million postage stamps, so as to do something definite before he died. Remember, you must always have your original

245

material — carefully noted down at the time of occurrence — with you, so that you may say in answer to his Why? Because of this, and this, and this.

However good may be the outfit for your work that you take with you, you will have, at first, great difficulty in realising that it is possible for the people you are among really to believe things in the way they do. And you cannot associate with them long before you must recognise that these Africans have often a remarkable mental acuteness and a large share of common sense; that there is nothing really "child-like" in their form of mind at all....

A careful study of the things a man, black or white, fails to do, whether for good or evil, usually gives you a truer knowledge of the man than the things he succeeds in doing....

The best protection lies in recognising the untrust-worthiness of human evidence regarding the unseen, and also the seen, when it is viewed by a person who has in his mind an explanation of the phenomenon before it occurs. For example, take a person who, believing in ghosts, sees a white figure in a churchyard, bolts home, has fits, and on revival states he has seen a ghost, and gives details. He has seen a ghost and therefore he is telling the truth. Another person who does not believe in ghosts sees the thing, flies at it and finds its component parts are boy and bed-sheet.

Do not applaud this individual, for he is quite conceited enough to make him comfortable; yet when he says the phenomenon was a boy and a bed-sheet, he is also telling the truth, and not much more of the truth than observer number one, for, after all, inside the boy there is a real ghost that made him go and do the thing. I know many people have doubts as to the existence of souls in small boys of this class, holding that they contain only devils; but devils can become ghosts, according to a mass of testimony.

Travels in West Africa, 434–441

Mary Kingsley's book, the result of her travels in West Africa in the 1890s, was widely read in England and elsewhere, and she was much in demand as a lecturer. She made at least three contributions of enormous importance to her home society. Her keen powers of observation, her meticulous notes, and her method of questioning widely held assumptions contributed to the methodology of her disciplines of ethnology and of botany and biology. She helped many of her countrymen come to a deeper and more sophisticated understanding of African life. She added to the store of knowledge about a variety of topics from fetish to fish.

 What have you learned, in content, in skills, in methodology that you will apply when you return home? In what ways? How might you help to dispel ignorance about your host culture?

 What "flags" — religion, political ideology, or other — have you had to lower to "bag your game" of understanding your host culture?

JANE ADDAMS

It is hard to tell just when the very simple plan which afterward developed into the Settlement began to form itself in my mind. It may have been even before I went to Europe for the second time, but I gradually became convinced that it would be a good thing to rent a house in a part of the city where many primitive and actual needs are found, in which young women who had been given over too exclusively to study, might restore a balance of activity along traditional lines and learn of life from life itself; where they might try out some of the things they had been taught and put truth to "the ultimate test of the conduct it dictates or inspires."

Twenty Years at Hull-House, 59

Jane Addams's idea of the settlement house brought together new immigrants and young middle-class people like herself who had had the advantages of higher education. Hull-House was to be an experiment in mutual aid and mutual education with each group benefiting, though in different ways, from the association.

 Service-learning is similar. What benefits has the experience brought to you?

 Have your presence and service, like those of the service-learning students who have gone before you, been a boon to those among whom you live and work? In what ways, and by what evidence do you judge it so?

 What "truths" have you put to the "test of conduct"? Which have stood up to the test and which have failed?

EMILY BRONSON CONGER

The bells, the first tones of which came down through that magnificent forest of huge trees and echoing from the rocks of that wonderful ravine, will ever sound in my ears as an instant call to a reverential mood. The solemn music was unlike any tone I had ever heard before; now it seemed the peal of the trumpet of the Last Day, now a call to some festival of angels and arch-angels. As the first thrills of emotion passed, it seemed a benediction of peace and rest; the evening's Gloria to the day's Jubilate, for it was the sunset hour....

I am not at all prepared to judge the Japanese creeds or modes of worship. But one may infer something of what people are taught, from their character and conduct. The children honor their parents; the women seem obedient to their husbands and masters; and the men are imbued with the love of country.

An Ohio Woman in the Philippines, 23, 27

Emily Bronson Conger was a devoted and committed Christian believer, yet she was able to worship her God in the shadow of the Shinto Shrine. She was also able to appreciate the values of Japanese culture, although admittedly it was within the framework of her own most precious values—family life and love of country. While not perfect or complete, Conger's empathy proved to be a boon for there is evidence that upon her return to San Francisco she helped many of her influential friends give up their distrust of the Japanese.

 Have you been able to appreciate, at least in part, the religious traditions and beliefs of your hosts? Have you seen anything which your own religion and that of your host hold in common?

 Are there values of your home culture that are evident in your host culture?

 What opinions do you expect to hear at home that run counter to your experience? How will you address the ignorance and xenophobia of those at home?

ANTHONY WINKLER

A streak of callousness ran in our people. It sprang from the capriciousness of our history, from the wearying and brutalizing poverty whose stench was constantly in the wind. Even in the countryside where the land was luxuriant and rich and where fruit grew bountifully everywhere the eye looked, we saw children with distended bellies, their bodies clothed in rags and tatters, their faces stamped with the whorls and scabs of ringworm. You passed disfigured men and women in the streets, some with the jellylike sac of a goitre slushing off their necks, others with the scars and sores that bespoke years of desperate neglect and want. The signs of hunger, hardship, need, were scribbled wantonly over the soiled black and brown faces everywhere you looked.

You did not see such sights in America where the people drifted past in the clean translucent aquariums of spacious malls looking as torpidly content as well-fed carp. Misery and pain existed there, too, but it had been swept into dark corners for tending by specialists.

But you could not escape seeing the poverty, the grinding want in a third world country such as Jamaica. To arrive at any shopping plaza in a motor car was to be surrounded by a cloud of unkempt beggars who flew at you from corners and walls with clamoring cries and grimy outstretched paws. To stop at a traffic light drew hordes of spindly urchins who swabbed your windshield with rags and sponges and then thrust a bony palm under your nose for money.

Want was everywhere, even in the opulent hotel in which you stayed, where it nibbled at the carpet, the bedsheets, the doormat like unseen vermin.

You could not avoid the sights and sounds of suffering. The wounded, the homeless, the mad shuffled to your very doorstep and bayed under your window.

My brother, for example, owned a palatial house on the brow of an affluent mountain suburb where even in a blistering summer the nights were freshened by a breeze. One morning on a walk I nearly stumbled over a madman crumpled in a dishevelled pile of bones and rags at the gate. He was muttering to himself, scribbling gibberish in the dirt and hardly looked up at the white man who calmly stepped out of the driveway for a morning stroll. You were torn between the impulse to gawk and cry, "My God, who did this terrible thing to you?" or mutter a polite "Good morning," and go about your business.

So a rind of insensibility hardened over your heart. You looked on misery and grief and found humour. You laughed at suffering, traded banter about the ghastly daily sights you had witnessed. As part of your tropical seasoning, you became almost religiously serene in your acceptance of horror.

Going Home to Teach, 220–221

Boon? Anthony Winkler describes as callous the reaction of affluent Jamaicans to the suffering around them. He observes that humor and "religiously serene acceptance" are common responses of those who encounter the poverty of others.

 What has happened to you as you have been involved in your agency and seen human suffering and need? What understanding will you bring home to others about issues of poverty, want, illness, and other human needs?

STAGE XI

CHARTING THE COURSE

As the story reaches the climax and the hero's thoughts turn to home, it is time for him to look at the road behind and ahead to see a pattern to the journey. Logic might suggest that mapping comes first; that we lay out the destination with predictable benchmarks before we begin a journey. But in most of the great legends the trail over which the hero has traveled becomes apparent only as the tale draws to an end. The hero, after all, is always exploring new territory. It has been the freedom to choose from different forks in the road, to follow the mysterious rhythm of leading and being led that finally reveals purpose and meaning and, some would say, destiny.

Now is the time to review the chart you have been making through your learning, your service, all of your other experiences and reflections, and from the journal itself. Recall where you started and trace how far you have come. Like Little Red Riding Hood, analyze how you have been misled. Face into your complaints, remembering perhaps the Boy Who Cried Wolf. Think about when you made up your mind precipitously and when you acted too timidly and, like the Greek nymph Daphne, missed an opportunity.

Are there themes that have emerged? Is there a pattern underneath? In the telling of the great hero legends, this is the point at which the griot reviews the journey, recapping the adventures and interpreting their meaning. Perhaps you wish to add to journal entries already made or enter new ones. Are you able to discern in what you have written central ideas or

253

interests about your host nation, your studies, your service, your career, your aspirations, your skills, your likes, your dislikes, or about the values you have been developing that will govern your future choices?

For many students, the last weeks of the service-learning experience bring clarity about why they entered the program, what they have learned, the challenges they have been presented, the beasts they have battled, and the gates they have flung open. They identify and express gratitude for the mentors and guardian spirits in the program and in their lives. Most of all, they give words to the victories won and boons they have discovered. They look with confidence to the road ahead.

But it is not so for all. Seeing the chart cannot be rushed and cannot, despite the best efforts of parents and schools, be imposed from without. You may now see the path behind and ahead clearly, or it may remain shrouded in mist, or—and this is the most likely—you see clearly one minute and find the clouds have returned the next. Perhaps you will see your journey not as a map, but only as a compass, providing general direction but no specific street names.

As the weeks and days of your international service-learning program draw to a close, chart where you are now as best you can. And, like the heroes of old, trust that as you have found your way thus far, so you will in the future as your life's direction unfolds.

JANE ADDAMS

As our boarding-school days neared the end, in the consciousness of approaching separation we vowed eternal allegiance to our "early ideals," and promised each other we would "never abandon them without conscious justification," and we often warned each other of "the perils of self-tradition."

We believed, in our sublime self-conceit, that the difficulty of life would lie solely in the direction of losing these precious ideals of ours, of failing to follow the way of martyrdom and high purpose we had marked out for ourselves, and we had no notion of the obscure paths of tolerance, just allowance, and self-blame wherein, if we held our minds open, we might learn something of the mystery and complexity of life's purposes.

The year after I had left college I came back, with a classmate, to receive the degree we had so eagerly anticipated. Two of the graduating class were also ready and four of us were dubbed B.A. on the very day that Rockford Seminary was declared a college in the midst of tumultuous anticipations. Having had a year outside of college walls in that trying land between vague hope and definite attainment, I had become very much sobered in my desire for a degree, and was already beginning to emerge from that rose-colored mist with which the dream of youth so readily envelops the future.

Whatever may have been the perils of self-tradition, I certainly did not escape them, for it required eight years — from the time I left Rockford in the summer of 1881 until Hull-House was opened in the autumn of 1889 — to formulate my convictions even in the least satisfactory manner, much less to reduce them to a plan for action. During most of that time I was absolutely at sea so far as any moral purpose was concerned, clinging only to the desire to live in a really living world and refusing to be content with a shadowy intellectual or aesthetic reflection of it.

Twenty Years at Hull-House, 45–46

Most heroes embark on their journeys from some level of discontent. Jane Addams admits that it took her eight years in which she was "absolutely at sea" about her purpose and direction. (Some would say she was blessed that it was *only* eight years.) But she did know her mind about wanting to "live in a really living world and refusing to be content with a showy intellectual or aesthetic reflection of it."

 You may not know exactly in which direction you will go, and it may even be hard at this point to see where you have been. But are you able to identify any ideas, attitudes, feelings or values about which you are clear that may point you in the direction that is right for you? Where do you stand regarding the relationship between formal academic learning and "a really living world?" Have the ideas and ideals which drew you to service-learning been changed in any way during your time in the program?

 Are there for you, as for Jane Addams, early ideals that you have moderated as a result of seeing mystery and complexity?

MARY KINGSLEY

I succumbed to the charm of the Coast as soon as I left Sierra Leone on my first voyage out, and I saw more than enough during that voyage to make me recognise that there was any amount of work for me worth doing down there. So I warned the Coast I was coming back again and the Coast did not believe me; and on my return to it a second time displayed a genuine surprise, and formed an even higher opinion of my folly than it had formed on our first acquaintance, which is saying a good deal.

During this voyage in 1893, I had been to Old Calabar, and its Governor, Sir Claude MacDonald, had heard me expatiating on the absorbing interest of the Antarctic drift, and the importance of the collection of fresh-water fishes and so on. So when Lady MacDonald heroically decided to go out to him in Calabar, they most kindly asked me if I would join her, and make my time fit hers for starting on my second journey. This I most willingly did, but I fear that very sweet and gracious lady suffered a great deal of apprehension at the prospect of spending a month on board ship with a person so devoted to science as to go down the West Coast in its pursuit. During the earlier days of our voyage she would attract my attention to all sorts of marine objects overboard, so as to amuse me. I used to look at them, and think it would be the death of me if I had to work like this, explaining meanwhile aloud that "they were very interesting, but Haeckel had done them, and I was out after fresh-water fishes from a river north of the Congo this time," fearing all the while that she felt me unenthusiastic for not flying over into the ocean to secure the specimens.

Travels in West Africa, 11–12

Mary Kingsley decided on the serious study of fresh-water fish and of fetish as a result of her first journey to West Africa, and found others anxious to aid her, though the help offered was often no help at all.

 Has your journey of service-learning abroad clarified your future either in eliminating possible interests or intensifying them? Are you finding real help in fulfilling your purpose or, as for Kingsley, only people of good will but no knowledge?

SAMUEL JOHNSON

Such are the things which this journey has given me the opportunity of seeing, and such are the reflections which that sight has raised. Having passed my time almost wholly in cities, I may have been surprized by modes of life and appearances of nature that are familiar to men of wider survey and more varied conversation. Novelty and ignorance must always be reciprocal, and I cannot but be conscious that my thoughts on national manners are the thought of one who has seen but little.

A Journey to the Western Islands of Scotland, 240

Samuel Johnson traveled in Scotland for eighty-five days. In his journal he recognizes that the time was short for reaching a profound appreciation of the country and culture.

 Johnson says that "novelty and ignorance must always be reciprocal." What does he mean?

 How do you assess the length of your program vis à vis your learning about the host culture? Did the combination of study and service enrich your understanding? Do you regret or are you glad that you stayed in one place rather than selecting a program of traveling from one place to another throughout your time abroad?

 Are there dimensions of your host community that you have not yet explored or fully understood? How long do you believe you would need to remain in order to learn these things?

 Do you hope one day to return to your host nation and community?

S ANA H ASAN

A mood of depression and despair began to settle in on me as the evening drew to a close. Perhaps it was the ceremony of the seder that highlighted for me the irony of a once homeless people now making others homeless. Or perhaps it was Danny's [marriage] proposal that weighed me down and intensified my confusion. The noise the soldiers were making, the buzz of their voices, the sight of their exhilaration, shook my nerves, and Gaza's proximity to the Egyptian border flooded me with memories of home. Here I could hardly escape ironies that were more personal. What was I doing here in Gaza, celebrating the Jewish people's ancient liberation from their Egyptian oppressors with a group of jolly Israeli soldiers who were the official occupying presence in Egyptian territory? I felt like a mass of broken fragments without a center. No matter what else I might have become, I was an Egyptian—but what was that? Again and again I sought to pull myself together and to look bright when Danny's eyes rested on my face, to tell myself that this day was the greatest of my life. But all I succeeded in doing was brooding over the feelings the whole celebration aroused in me, and still more over those I would have liked to feel but could not....

And then there was Danny. I knew that leaving the country was the only way of severing my emotional ties with him, since I did not have the willpower to be near him without seeing him. But if I finally summoned up enough courage to leave, it was because I realized that my attachment to Danny was symptomatic of the chilling isolation in which my broadened sympathy for Israel had placed me. I needed to return to the safety of my known identity as a Harvard student; I needed the comfortable distance that separated me, the political activist for peace, from Israel. Above all, I needed to go home, to Egypt, to find myself again.

Enemy in the Promised Land, 322–323, 326

One can imagine no journey that exposed the traveler to a more diametrically opposite set of beliefs than did Egyptian Sana Hasan's trip to Israel. And there she had the fortune — or misfortune — to fall in love with an Israeli army officer. She knew she had to choose between the man she loved and her family and heritage.

 Have you had to struggle in any way between new and old loyalties? Have you, in any way, come to a fork in the road? Which direction will you take?

PAUL COWAN

We must have talked about the possibility of leaving Guayaquil every single day during those months. (I was just about to turn twenty-six, so the draft was no longer a problem.) I remember one particularly depressing afternoon in August when Rachel and I sat in the riverfront park near the statue of Bolivar and San Martin, each of us pushing the other toward tears as we dwelled obsessively on our failures and frustrations. (It was the week that Jerry Rubin transformed the House Un-American Activities Committee from a threat into a joke by testifying in a Revolutionary War costume.) We were almost as troubled by the attitude that most volunteers had adopted toward us as by the fact that we had no job. Most people in our group felt that because we lived in a virtual mansion while we criticized the Peace Corps and the work it had assigned us we were hypocrites, unable to live by the standards we had invoked so often in training. Instead of helping the poor, we were demoralizing the other volunteers. One physical-education specialist talked openly about his great desire to "knock Paul Cowan out." Even Bill and Joyce Dodge and Ralph Craft, who agreed with the majority of our criticisms of the Peace Corps, seemed to feel that my intensity was unseemly, perhaps a little crazy, and that Rachel was not the same sweet person she had been just a few months earlier. Nick and Margot were our only real friends.

But we couldn't bring ourselves to quit the Peace Corps, for that act would be an admission of personal failure. In a way, the organization continued to hold the same mythic sway over our minds it had when we'd joined. The more deeply we hated it, the more determined we became to succeed on terms its members could accept.

To a very great extent, our self-respect depended on our ability to find useful work in Guayaquil and to change the Peace

Corps so that it would be more responsive to the needs of the Ecuadorians and the feelings of the volunteers.

The Making of an Un-American, 239–240

Conflicting feelings produce confusion about what route to follow. Paul Cowan's dilemma came from a combination of his political opinions, his relations with other Peace Corps volunteers, and his own sense of responsibility to complete successfully what he had started.

 Have you felt tempted to quit? What would leaving such a project or program have done to your self-esteem and to the project?

 Every day you made decisions about the way you would spend your time. As you come to the end of your program and look back on these daily decisions, how do you assess the road you traveled? Did you make wise decisions? Are you proud of the path you took? Do you see the cumulative effect of the daily decisions you made to study and to serve?

K<small>ATHLEEN</small> N<small>ORRIS</small>

There are those born and raised here who can't imagine living anywhere else. There are also those who are drawn here — teachers willing to take the lowest salaries in the nation; clergy with theological degrees from Princeton, Cambridge, and Zurich who want to serve small rural churches — who find that they cannot remain for long. Their professional mobility sets them apart and becomes a liability in an isolated Plains community where outsiders are treated with an uneasy mix of hospitality and rejection.

Dakota: A Spiritual Geography, 6–7

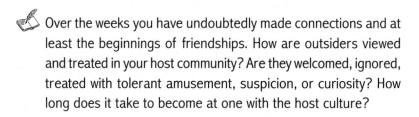 Over the weeks you have undoubtedly made connections and at least the beginnings of friendships. How are outsiders viewed and treated in your host community? Are they welcomed, ignored, treated with tolerant amusement, suspicion, or curiosity? How long does it take to become at one with the host culture?

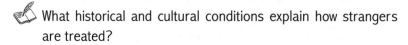 What historical and cultural conditions explain how strangers are treated?

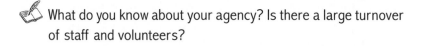 As in the Dakotas, do strangers who come to serve in your host community eventually leave?

What do you know about your agency? Is there a large turnover of staff and volunteers?

The road a hero decides to take is determined within the privacy of his own mind and heart, but the behavior of others towards him contributes significantly to his decision. What attitudes towards you have had a part in determining your direction?

SAMUEL JOHNSON

I sat down on a bank, such as a writer of Romance might have delighted to Feign. I had indeed no trees to whisper over my head, but a clear rivulet streamed at my feet. The day was calm, the air soft, and all was rudeness, silence, and solitude. Before me, and on either side, were high hills, which by hindering the eye from ranging, forced the mind to find entertainment for itself. Whether I spent the hour well I know not; for here I first conceived the thought of this narration.

We were in this place at ease and by choice, and had no evils to suffer or to fear; yet the imaginations excited by the view of an unknown and untravelled wilderness are not such as arise in the artificial solitude of parks and gardens, a flattering notion of self-sufficiency, a placid indulgence of voluntary delusions, a secure expansion of the fancy, or a cool concentration of the mental powers. The phantoms which haunt a desert are want, and misery, and danger; the evils of dereliction rush upon the thoughts; man is made unwillingly acquainted with his own weakness, and meditation show him only how little he can sustain, and how little he can perform. There were no traces of inhabitants, except perhaps a rude pile of clods called a summer hut, in which a herdsman had rested in the favorable seasons. Whoever had been in the place where I then sat, unprovided with provisions and ignorant of the country, might, at least before the roads were made, have wandered among the rocks, till he had perished with hardship, before he could have found either food or shelter. Yet what are these hillocks to the ridges of Taurus, or these spots of wildness to the deserts of America?

Johnson and Boswell, 89

Samuel Johnson claims to have had the thought for the book (narration) while sitting on a river's bank in Scotland. But can anyone seriously believe that such a prolific writer would not have had the thought of writing before he began the trip to the Western Hebrides, or that gaining material about which to write was the chief motivation for his travels?

His very choice of wild and barren Scotland for his first trip abroad, rather than the more popular destinations of France or Italy, was reflective of his interests in nature and environmental issues and of his reflective manner which, he freely admits, Scotland furthered.

 Where do you do your best thinking? Why do you think you selected the location you did rather than another? What can you see in yourself that directs your choices and course? Can you see this more clearly now that you near the end of your program than you did before you embarked? Have you learned more about yourself and further refined or defined who you are and want to be?

 What has the experience of journal writing been like for you? A pleasure, anticipated or unexpected? A chore? Is it the thinking about the issues or the writing itself that is the joy or the burden?

ANTHONY WINKLER

The Canadian math instructor, Mendoza, who to my mind provides a mini-moral to this tale, fared better than Jameson. Mendoza was mercenary; Mendoza was avaricious; Mendoza was uncharitable. Mendoza despised Manley and socialism, stoutly rejected the gospel that every man was his brother's keeper. She was keeper solely of her loved ones and laboured only for gain that would better their private lot. Yet Mendoza outlasted every foreign tutor who has ever taught at Longstreet out of philanthropy or humanitarian love. She did not serve merely a year or two as did itinerant missionaries such as Evelyn Moon or global nomads such as Peter Matheson. Mendoza taught at Longstreet for ten rich and productive years. Worldly gain, pure and simple, was her only motive, and for this grubby reason she trained hundreds of teachers and bequeathed the school the legacy of an innovative math curriculum. Years after I had served my own fleeting altruistic term at Longstreet, Mendoza remained behind doing useful work.

Her career in Jamaica ended on a stroke of happenstance and bad luck. One day a bureaucrat in Ottawa accidentally stumbled on her file and gasped, "Good God! We've been paying this teacher all these years under the wrong scale!" Mendoza's salary was cut to the prevailing missionary pittance. She immediately resigned, sold her mansion to the fiery socialist Raymond Hunt, and left Jamaica.

Mendoza's story is rich with biblical paradox and offers a tentative explanation of why socialism failed in Jamaica, of why Manley's well-meaning and humane government was so bungled and futile. Manley failed because his socialism lacked the attraction of betterment.

Betterment was what Mendoza found in Jamaica, what kept her there. When she left Jamaica she was richer by far than when she had come. Betterment of this sort is what human beings universally want for themselves and their loved ones.

The idealistic appeals of socialism that call for unselfish sacrifice in exchange for the collective betterment of one's nation are too remote and monastic to stir ordinary hearts. Humans crave betterment that is personal, exact, measurable in teaspoons. Yes, yes, we want a better nation; but first we want a better hat. Many scowling Russian old men find this lust ugly and rage against it, but the craving to better oneself is in the blood and will persist to the end of humanity's days.

Going Home to Teach, 264–265

Anthony Winkler suggests that the road to success in rendering real service may not lie in the direction of idealism, humanitarianism, or altruism, but rather in the hard-nosed and hardheaded desire for personal achievement and gain.

 What do you think of his analysis?

Winkler cites the Manley government's denial of the desire for betterment as a reason Jamaica failed to make significant economic gains.

 Can you cite instances related to the desire for betterment that retarded or advanced progress in the life of your host nation?

 What experiences have you had with fellow staff members at your agency? Who has succeeded and who has failed in their jobs at the agency in which you are serving? How do you explain their success or failure?

 Can you identify your motivations in the past, during the program and for the future? What has kept you on the path of service?

LANGSTON HUGHES

When spring came, and the banks of the Hudson were a fresh, clean green, and the New York–Albany boats appeared on the river, I thought it was about time to leave the dead ships and find a vessel that was moving. So I quit the fleet and went back to New York, determined now to get on a boat actually going somewhere. It didn't take long. My red-headed steward gave me a splendid recommendation: "Competent, courteous, capable, trust-worthy, and efficient." So I took his letter to a shipping office and that very day was assigned a boat sailing for Africa—providing the Filipino steward didn't mind a Negro in his crew. He didn't, so I got the job.

I'd left a box of books in Harlem in the fall, and before we sailed I went after them. I brought them aboard ship with me. But when I opened them up and looked at them that night off Sandy Hook, they seemed too much like everything I had known in the past, like the attics and basements in Cleveland, like the lonely nights in Toluca, like the dormitory at Columbia, like the furnished room in Harlem, like too much reading all the time when I was a kid, like life isn't as described in romantic prose; so that night, I took them all out on deck and threw them overboard. It was like throwing a million bricks out of my heart—for it wasn't only the books that I wanted to throw away, but everything unpleasant and miserable out of my past: the memory of my father, the poverty and uncertainties of my mother's life, the stupidities of color-prejudice, black in a white world, the fear of not finding a job, the bewilderment of no one to talk to about things that trouble you, the feeling of always being controlled by others—by parents, by employers, by some outer necessity not your own. All those things I wanted to throw away. To be free of. To escape from. I wanted to be a man on my own, control my own life, and go my own way. I was twenty-one. So I threw the books in the sea.

The Big Sea, 97–98

This Langston Hughes passage should have a familiar ring. The same story, told by Hughes in different words, appears in the second stage, "Departing and Separating." Hughes offers these two versions, the first to begin his autobiography and the second to end its first section. It represents the end of his preparation and childhood and marks his entry into adulthood. It is the moment when he decided he must chart his course for himself rather than try to satisfy either his parents (who were pulling him in two different directions) or the academic establishment.

 Where are you in the process of making decisions for yourself? Have you faced opposition to any direction you wish to take or have taken? What might you throw away, as Hughes did his books, that is a symbol of your former self?

STAGE XII

RETURNING HOME

With battles fought and won, mysteries encountered and unshrouded, boons discovered and captured, new territory covered and mapped, the hero turns in the direction of home.

The return journey is never a mere retracing of steps. Some heroes take a new route home, prolonging their adventure. But even for those who choose the now-familiar road, the return is a new experience enveloped in new meaning.

For most returning heroes, the return is filled with intense and sometimes contradictory feelings — eagerness to be reunited with friends and family, sadness that the adventure and the relationships that were part of it are coming to an end, and relief that the mission has been accomplished. Even after the best of journeys made by the most adventurous of heroes, there is a welcome end to the stress of living in a foreign land and traveling a road not fully known. Of course, a few travelers choose not to return, adopting the foreign land as their own or wandering forever.

But most heroes, arriving home, begin to share the news of the journey, the victories won and the boons discovered. Companions listen with interest and admiration.

But it is not always so. The returning hero has been changed — Joseph Campbell would say transfigured — and he may feel out of joint with those at home. He has moved beyond the confines of his previous existence, and found new wisdom, a new vocation, new friends, and new mentors. Old comrades may remain unchanged or have moved in different directions. Parents have gotten older, grandparents may have died, childhood homes sold or redecorated, younger siblings no longer children. In his absence, the hero's girlfriend may have found a new love. These changes may require considerable adjustment as the hero shifts his expectations of his return to meet the reality he finds there.

But even beyond the external changes is the deeper one of the new role that the adventurer-hero has now assumed. No hero returns feeling the same about self as before departure, nor should she. Having traveled to new realms, met challenges, conquered beasts, blazed trails, gained new insights, and developed skills, the returning traveler finds that more is expected of her than before the journey began. She perceives herself as more adult and is perceived by others as a leader, looked to for new knowledge, sought after for advice, expected to assume the responsibility that such a position in society entails. If this change is not recognized and acknowledged by family and friends, the hero experiences disappointment and rejection.

In many cultures, the experience of the journey is ritualized in rites of passage. The young person who reaches a certain age is taken away from family and village, put through a rigorous period of training and testing under the direction of special mentors. When the initiate returns, there may be a ceremony of bathing and dressing and a crowning with laurels, symbolizing the new person she has become. Persephone returns from the unknown world, now clothed in the garments of Spring. No longer considered a child, the young person is now publicly acknowledged as ready for the responsibilities and privileges of adulthood.

To his new position the hero will respond appropriately, accepting the mantle now placed on his shoulders. Just as he responded to the call to embark on the hero's journey, so now he accepts the consequences, assenting with willing mind and heart to the tasks now given, now chosen, and looking forward to the new world of challenge, opportunity, and difference that lies ahead.

SANA HASAN

There was something uncanny about returning home after eight years only to find that my own people mistook me for a foreigner, as though my inner changes were somehow reflected in my physical appearance. I noticed that the town too had changed: It seemed smaller — or was it simply that there were more people in Cairo, masses of people wedged in at the crossings? There seemed to be no forward movement to them; even the air felt stale, all but exhausted. Finally we reached the bridge, and the imposing buildings that carried the comforting names of my childhood: Park Lane, Dorchester, Nile View. These venerable buildings were the Cairo I knew; they were my past. They had stood there, immovable and dignified, during all those years when I had scorned them as bourgeois artifacts and relics of a colonial past best forgotten. Now they brought tears to my eyes. But any hopes I had of recapturing the past and my place in it were soon dashed. I had returned to a different world.

I hardly recognized my own neighborhood. What two decades of Nasser's "socialist" revolution had not succeeded in accomplishing, Sadat had brought about in a few years with his "Open-Door" policy. The old, impoverished aristocracy had been run out of Zamalek by hordes of Egyptian nouveaux riches and Japanese and Western businessmen. This once exclusive island now resembled any downtown area, with the same congested streets and the same rubbish-strewn sidewalks.

Even my home seemed foreign to me. Gone were the Louis XV brocade chairs. In their place had come modern furniture. Since the salons were seldom used these days, the settees and armchairs were covered with sheets of linen meant to keep the dust off the pale, raw silk upholstery. These lent the rooms the lugubrious look of an apartment in which someone had just died. I went back and forth between the marble stand with the statuette of Cupid and the little round table that supported porcelain bonbonières, enameled cigarette boxes, and ashtrays of solid silver, as well as a bouquet of flowers fashioned of delicate bits of irregular colored glass, and the Sèvres hunting dog in black and white. I had always made fun of these useless objects; now I found comfort in their presence.

Enemy in the Promised Land, 232–233

Sana Hasan had remained in Israel for eight years. She had changed enormously and so, she discovered, had her home in Cairo.

 Has anyone failed to recognize you upon your return, or commented on your change in appearance or behavior?

Hasan's adolescent view was that her home was bourgeois and colonial: upon return she found herself sympathetic to and comforted by the very things she had previously scorned.

 Are you finding that places and things now mean something different to you than they did in the past?

 Her neighborhood had changed with the political changes. Do you see differences in your town, city, neighborhood? What is new, gone, renovated, neglected? What is the cause of these changes?

EMILY BRONSON CONGER

On reaching San Francisco the ship was placed in quarantine the usual number of days, but there was no added delay as there were on board no cases of infectious disease. Mrs. General Funston was one of the passengers and was greeted most cordially by the friends and neighbors of this, her native state. Upon my declaring to the custom house officers that I had been two years in the Philippines and had nothing for sale they immediately passed my baggage without any trouble. My son in New York, to whom I had cabled from Nagasaki, had never received my message, so there was no one to meet me, but I was so thankful to be in dear, blessed America that it was joy enough. No, not enough until I reached my own beloved home. Had it been possible I would have kissed every blade of grass on its grounds, and every leaf on its trees.

I am not ashamed to say that July 10th, the day of my home coming, I knelt down and kissed with unspeakable gratitude and love its dear earth and once more thanked God that His hand had led me—led me home.

An Ohio Woman in the Philippines, 166

Patriotic American that she was, Emily Conger was glad to be back in the United States. But it was her house—her home—that was the chief object of her affection and gratitude.

 What place do you cherish and most look forward to returning to? What experiences, relationships, values or beliefs does it represent? Who will be there? Do you anticipate that the place or the people will have changed?

Langston Hughes

In the late summer I began to make ready to leave for Columbia. In Toluca the schools had vacation at odd times, so most of my English classes continued throughout the summer. I hated to leave them, but I told Señorita Padilla and Professor Tovar that they would have to find someone else [to teach].

A short time later, Professor Tovar told me he had learned that a new American couple had come to Toluca, a road engineer and his wife, and that the woman was willing to take over my English classes. I was glad, because the two Mexican teachers of English I had met there had a good knowledge of grammar, but atrocious pronunciation.

While I went for a final trip to the ranch with my father, Professor Tovar and Señorita Padilla called on the American woman and made final arrangements with her to take over the girls' school and business school classes. They set a day for her to come to the business school in the Portales to go over the lessons with me, and to visit the commercial classes.

Professor Tovar had neglected to tell the new teacher that I was an *americano de color,* brown as a Mexican, and nineteen years old. So when she walked into the room with him, she kept looking around for the American teacher. No doubt she thought I was one of the students, chalk in hand, standing at the board. But when she was introduced to me, her mouth fell open, and she said: "Why Ah-Ah thought you was an American."

I said: "I am American!"

She said: "Oh, Ah mean a white American!" Her voice had a southern drawl.

I grinned.

She was a poor-looking lady of the stringy type, who probably had never been away from her home town before. I asked her what part of the States she came from. She said Arkansas—which better explained her immediate interest in color. The next two days, as she sat beside me at the teacher's desk, and I went over with her the different types of courses the students had — the conversation for the girls from Señorita Padilla's school, and the business English for the pupils of the academy — she kept looking at me out of the corners of her eyes as if she thought maybe I might bite her.

At the end of the first day, she said: "Ah never come across an educated Ne-gre before." (Southerners often make that word a slur between *nigger* and *Negro.)*

I said: "They have a large state college for colored people in Arkansas, so there must be some educated ones there."

She said: "Ah reckon so, but Ah just never saw one before." And she continued to gaze at me as her first example of an educated Negro.

I was a bit loath to leave my students, with whom I had had so much fun, in charge of a woman from one of our more backward states, who probably felt about brown Mexicans much as my father did. But there was no alternative, if they wanted to learn English at all. Then, too, I thought the young ladies from Señorita Padilla's academy might as well meet a real *gringo* for once. Feminine gender: *gringa.*

The Big Sea, 77–79

Langston Hughes had loved his teaching in Mexico and his pupils. Now it was time for him to leave them to another teacher, one whom he thought less qualified than he, with poor skills and an even worse attitude.

 Who will take over the job you have been doing? How do you feel about leaving your job in another's hands? Did you do anything to smooth the transition?

PAUL COWAN

The cheapest place to eat in Bogotá was the cafeteria of the National University, the most radical school in the country, and the next day everyone on our trip went there for lunch. From the start the atmosphere seemed unusually volatile. As we were standing in line I noticed a great deal of whistling and some stamping, though I assumed that it was just some students impatient to eat. Then, in the dining room, I was conscious of people staring at me, but I figured that, like so many Latins, they were amused by my height and by the sweat that so often pours off my face. So I ignored them. I concentrated on a conversation in which Rachel and I were trying to persuade Father Roen, who still supported the war [in Vietnam], that the CIA was implicated in the assassination of Ngo Diem Dinh.

But I had a headache, and I went up to the counter to buy an aspirin. As I headed back to our table, I began to hear a great clatter. People were banging on their plates, their cups, their chairs: any hard object. And yelling!—in English and Spanish, "*Yanqui, go home,*" "*Afuera, Cuerpo de Paz,*" "*Abaio imperialismo.*" I saw one of the Ecuadorian students restraining a Colombian who was about to throw a bottle at me.

I suppose that James Meredith, walking through the dining hall at Ole Miss, must have felt the same nervousness as I did at National University. Only Meredith was the good guy.

Well, I thought for a moment, I'll not only be the bad guy, I'll embody evil. I'll give a Peace Corps speech! say what most volunteers would feel in that situation. "You ungrateful sons of camps! We've come down to train you in how to behave, and now you want to run us out of your dining room. Spic bastards! Too stupid to see what I can do for you. You know, the Marines have invaded entire countries for less than this. Just wait until I get back to America and go into the State Department. Then I'll have power over your miserable lives."

A real John Wayne speech, uncensored. Did Richard Nixon have similar thoughts when the students stoned his car in Caracas?

If I'd had the nerve to give that speech I would have provoked the kind of anti-American riot that I believe should sweep the continent.

Instead, I returned to my table, trying to look as calm as possible, and continued to chat with Rachel and Father Roen until the shouting ended. Then we got up to leave and the noise resumed, louder than ever. If I am ever trampled because of my beliefs, I decided, I want it to come after a confrontation with my real enemies, not political allies who don't know me.

At Choate I had learned that if you turn your back on taunts, and seem stubbornly docile, you are relatively safe. For the first time I put that coward's lesson to sensible use. Fortunately, we had been eating near an exit so we didn't have to pass many people on our way out the door. Soon the bus we had rented came to carry us to freedom.

"Don't take it personally," one of the Colombian students said as we were leaving the university. "To them you are not Paul and Rachel Cowan, two special people who are doing a special job. You are symbols of a government that is exploiting this country. If I hadn't known you I would have been yelling, too."

Everyone who was listening to the conversation, Ecuadorians as well as Colombians, said that they agreed.

Take it personally! In a way, my friends, that was the moment I had been waiting for ever since my Peace Corps group first arrived in Guayaquil. Nick had said, " '*Yanqui,* go home' is the most lucid piece of political theory that has ever been devised in this century." I agreed. The angry cries of the Colombian students exhilarated me. They reminded me that there must be tens of millions of people throughout the continent who wanted us to help them put that theory into practice.

Those cries told me that we must go home soon, too, and carry our fight with our own kind from a remote outpost of America to its decaying core.

The Making of an Un-American, 360–362

Paul Cowan concluded that despite his good intentions he had no business being in Latin America under the auspices of the U.S. government. He determined that the best arena for him in which to wage war against injustice was in his home territory.

 What have you concluded about your service and learning abroad? Was it good that you were there? What do you hope and plan to do when you return to further the cause(s) for which you were working in your host nation?

ANTHONY WINKLER

The Christmas holidays came and we flew to Cathy's hometown of Cicero, a suburb of Chicago. A few days before we left, my students trooped up the hill through the darkened pastures and serenaded us with carols. They stood in the seine of light shining through the burglar-barred windows of our cottage and chorused in the dimness. Then they came inside and we sang and celebrated with an early Christmas party.

In Cathy's hometown of Cicero, which had been settled mainly by Eastern Europeans, everywhere I looked — in the restaurants, the malls, on the streets — I saw an ocean of white skin, Slavic cheekbones, enormous skulls, and simian limbs. The houses are squat and ugly like abandoned bunkers, stained with the colour of dried egg yoke, and crowned by a ridiculous facade of crenellated roofs. They stand side by side in gnomically gloomy rows, as indistinguishable as toadstools, each fondling a ribbon of sidewalk with a grimy stoop. Driven like a spike between each house is a narrow cement gangway where old ladies can be glimpsed peeping out suspiciously at the world from tiny backyard gardens. The entire town seemed crushed under a brutal ugliness.

But it was a relief to be nothing more than another inconspicuous white face in the crowd. And it was exhilarating to see the shelves of stores bursting with goods. Democratic socialism had so impoverished Jamaica that it was common to walk into a Kingston grocery and face aisle after aisle of naked shelving and ugly rivets. But here the shelves of grocers groaned under sacks of rice, sugar, flour; display windows twinkled gaily with Christmas lights; shops and stores and malls overflowed with consumer goods.

It took our breath away at first — the sheer, dazzling, breathless opulence of America. We had forgotten its richness, its variety, its sprightliness and energy. Plenty was all around us: conspicuous, shameless, intoxicating Plenty that goaded us to wallow and revel and joyously spend. This is what an immigrant first sniffs in the American breeze. It was the scent that had made me light-headed when I first stepped off the plane in Miami some thirteen years ago: Plenty, wafting on the air like the dizzying scent of spring after a gloomy winter.

In Manley's Jamaica a longing for Plenty made you feel like a masturbating schoolboy, made you want to skulk as if you concealed a secret sin. You had fallen prey to a debased craving, a sick appetite. Poverty was upright and holy and when it died would go straight to heaven like a righteous nanny. But Plenty was a painted whore and if you kept her company you stood naked and with your exposed nasty erection before choiring multitudes in a cathedral.

But I found myself asking: what was wrong with Plenty? What deranged theology was this, that made Human Want seem righteous, but Plenty wicked? Manley never came right out and said so, but this equation was implicit in every scolding utterance of democratic socialism that had lately made life in Jamaica insufferably straitlaced. It was as if the humourless Franciscan nuns at Mount Alvernia Academy, where I had gone to school in Montego Bay, now held sway over the country with their merciless Latin conjugations and smugly triumphant virginity.

It was a refreshing interlude for us—those three weeks in Cicero. We bought. We spent. We splurged without remorse. My attitude was, Piss on Socialism: here was a land where rice could be plucked with an indifferent hand off the shelf of any corner grocer, where flour, soap and cooking oil did not have to be hoarded or purchased with furtive premeditation. American money was all you needed to go on a spending binge, and we had twenty thousand dollars of it piled up in banks from textbook royalties. Cathy shopped for gifts and clothes. I bought books for my A level students. We revelled and danced practically every night.

A long time ago my father had visited America, and it had struck him then very much the same way that I was now affected.

Going Home to Teach, 174–175

The difference in affluence between one's home and the country visited is often the most immediate difference the returning traveler notices.

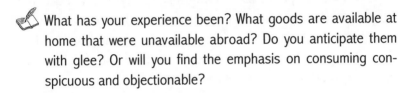 What has your experience been? What goods are available at home that were unavailable abroad? Do you anticipate them with glee? Or will you find the emphasis on consuming conspicuous and objectionable?

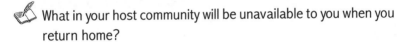 What in your host community will be unavailable to you when you return home?

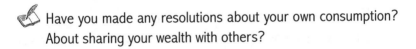 Have you made any resolutions about your own consumption? About sharing your wealth with others?

KATHLEEN NORRIS

When a friend referred to the western Dakotas as the Cappadocia of North America, I was handed an essential connection between the spirituality of the landscape I inhabit and that of the fourth-century monastics who set up shop in Cappadocia and the deserts of Egypt. Like those monks, I made a counter-cultural choice to live in what the rest of the world considers a barren waste. Like them, I had to stay in this place, like a scarecrow in a field, and hope for the brains to see its beauty. My idea of what makes a place beautiful had to change, and it has. The city no longer appeals to me for the cultural experiences and possessions I might acquire there, but because its population is less homogenous than Plains society. Its holiness is to be found in being open to humanity in all its diversity. And the western Plains now seem bountiful in their emptiness, offering solitude and room to grow.

Dakota: A Spiritual Geography, 3

Kathleen Norris is our one journalist who did not return, but rather chose to stay in the place to which she traveled, there to make her home and life. She says that in choosing the western plains instead of one of America's great cities she was making a "counter-cultural" choice.

 Have you considered not returning? What choices have you made that go against the prevailing culture and values?

 Norris changed her ideas about her previous home in New York City, and about the Great Plains which she made home. What perceptions of home have changed for you? Have the qualities you value in home changed as a result of living in a new country, community, and culture?

MARY KINGSLEY

The next few days I spent expecting the *Nachtigal*. Of course I had unpacked all my things again and most of them were at the wash, when Idabea rushes into my room saying, "*Nachtigal kommt*," and I packed furiously, and stood by to go aboard, having been well educated by my chief tutor, Captain Murray, on the iniquity of detaining the ship. I hasten to say the lesson on this point I never brought down on myself. I have never robbed a church or committed a murder, so should never dream of plunging into this lowermost depth of crime without a preparatory course of capital offences. When, however, I was packed, I found that it was not the *Nachtigal* which had come in, but the *Hyoena* — the guard-ship of Cameroons River — out for an airing, and as her commander Captain Baham, kindly asked me on board to lunch, I had to unpack again. At lunch I had the honour of meeting the two officers who had first ascended the peak of Cameroon from the south-east face, and I learnt from them many things which would have been of great help to me had I had this honour before I went up, but which were none the less good to know; and during the whole of their stay in Ambas Bay I received from the *Hyoena* an immense amount of pleasure, courtesy, and kindness, adding to the already great debt in these things I owe to Cameroons — a debt which I shall never forget, although I can never repay it.

The third announcement of the *Nachtigal* proved true, and with my dilapidated baggage I went round.

Travels in West Africa, 626–627

No matter how well we plan our leave-taking, something is bound to go wrong. These anti-climactic events remind us that even those who have been on a hero's journey are not, finally, in complete control. And, like Mary Kingsley, we often learn things at the last minute that it would have been good to know earlier. The hero's path is seldom straight.

 What were the final days, the good-byes, and the return journey like for you? Were there lessons learned and conclusions drawn?

 What debt do you owe to your host community that you can never repay?

JANE ADDAMS

A horde of perplexing questions, concerning those problems of existence of which in happier moments we catch but fleeting glimpses and at which we even then stand aghast, pursued us relentlessly on the long journey through the great wheat plains of South Russia, through the crowded Ghetto of Warsaw, and finally into the smiling fields of Germany where the peasant men and women were harvesting the grain. I remember that through the sight of those toiling peasants, I made a curious connection between the bread labor advocated by Tolstoy and the comfort the harvest fields are said to have once brought to Luther when, much perturbed by many theological difficulties, he suddenly forgot them all in a gush of gratitude for mere bread, exclaiming, "How it stands, that golden yellow corn, on its fine tapered stem; the meek earth, at God's kind bidding, has produced it once again!" At least the toiling poor had this comfort of bread labor....

I may have wished to secure this solace for myself at the cost of the least possible expenditure of time and energy, for during the next month in Germany, when I read everything of Tolstoy's that had been translated into English, German, or French, there grew up in my mind a conviction that what I ought to do upon my return to Hull-House, was to spend at least two hours every morning in the little bakery which we had recently added to the equipment of our coffee-house....

I held fast to the belief that I should do this, through the entire journey homeward, on land and sea, until I actually arrived in Chicago when suddenly the whole scheme seemed to me as utterly preposterous as it doubtless was. The half dozen people invariably waiting to see me after breakfast, the piles of letters to be opened and answered, the demand of actual and pressing human wants, — were these all to be pushed aside and asked to wait while I saved my soul by two hours' work at baking bread?

Twenty Years at Hull-House, 180–181

How often we, like Jane Addams, make resolutions for our lives when we are away from the press of daily responsibilities, only to find these intentions swamped when we return to school or job! Sometimes, as was true for Addams, we change our minds about what is really important, and we decide that our plans were but romantic dreams.

 What resolutions have you made for your life as a result of what you have seen, learned, and reflected upon while in the service-learning program? What obstacles do you face at home which will make it hard to keep your resolve?

Afterward / Foreward

by Howard A. Berry
President of The International Partnership for Service-Learning

> "Each hero's journey begins with a call to leave behind the familiar and to venture into parts unknown. The call may come suddenly ... or it may unfold gradually.... The call may be clearly recognized or but dimly perceived."

You began charting your own journey by reading these words. What, then, are they doing here at the end? They are here because there is one more important realization for you before you journey on.

Life is a process. Beginnings and endings are blurred, and blend into each other. Often the process is not even linear. Memories of the past come to us in the midst of new ventures and shape what we are doing and thinking. And new experiences allow us to revisit, reshape, and reinterpret what we have done before. The process of living becomes a continuous and organic whole, not a machine with separate parts and compartments.

You may have gone on your journey through an international service-learning experience, or you may have used this journal equally well to help you through another sort of life experience, charting and recording it by using this guide. Whatever the case, you are likely deservedly proud of yourself. You have separated, met challenges, battled the beasts, dealt with setbacks, celebrated the victories, discovered the boon, and returned home. You might feel that your journey has ended — except that it hasn't.

On your return you may have noticed that things, family, friends have changed. But mostly that is not so. It is *you* who have changed. You have grown, intellectually and emotionally. You see the world, and those you know, through new eyes and with new perceptions. You now know things you didn't know before. You may not even realize how much because these things have become an integral part of your thinking and seeing.

The journey you have taken will lead you to another one because now, thanks to this journal, your eye is sharper, your ear more finely tuned. As with music, the more we hear a song, a passage or a symphony, the more we hear in it. From what at first was noise and too many sounds to hear at the same time, with training and experience we begin to distinguish clearly the instruments, the harmonies, melodies, and tones.

You will hear the Call again, but like a musician you will recognize its notes more clearly. It may come to you loudly, with a full orchestral sound, or you may hear it as the quiet solo of a single instrument. Either way, or in whatever form, you will know it, and you will know that it is calling you to another journey.

You may, in fact, hear more than one Call, because the pattern of the journey remains the same, whether it is the Call to a career, a profession, a relationship you enter, or community service. At times you may need to decide which Call to heed — or perhaps not to respond at all. But now you will know you have been called, and will have at least some idea of what lies ahead.

You will also know the pattern of the journey. It will not, however, be a repetition. Although the Hero's Journey is ongoing, you will now experience it at a different level. Having journeyed once, your understanding will be fuller, more rounded, more dimensional.

Your journal, too, can change. You may certainly use this version and its wonderful traveling companions for future journeys but, excitingly, you can also design and create your own. The patterns and stages will remain, but you can change your companions by adding other writings from literature, history, and autobiography. You can develop your own questions, which will become more sophisticated, and perhaps more probing. You are not only an active learner in your own experiences, but you can now also create your own chart and your own story.

There is yet another possible, and equally important, role for you. The Call will come to you, but at the same time you may be the Herald for someone else, the voice that urges them on to take their first steps on the Journey. Or perhaps you will be the Mentor guiding another already engaged in the Journey. This is the continuity and coherence of the Hero's Journey, and what makes it universal and ongoing.

We at The International Partnership for Service-Learning hope, of course, that your future journeys will involve service, whether or not your first one did. We hope your experience of the Hero's Journey will stimulate in you what the author Robert Bellah has called "Habits of the Heart"—habits that lead you to a continuing concern with community, with those in need, and with the human condition.

Whatever your choices, whatever the directions you take, you are now aware that there are no ends, only new beginnings. And you now understand why we can say in this final word of the journal, as we did in the introduction, bon voyage.

And it made me braver,
And it made me taller,
And it made me tremble,
And it made me smaller,
And it made me ramble,
And it made me laugh and cry.

And it made me holler,
And it made me quiver,
And it made me fearless,
And it made me stumble,
And it made me foolish,
And it made me vanish,

And it made me want to fly
Out of myself
And into the Hidden Sky.

— from the musical The Hidden Sky,
by Peter Foley and Kate Chisholm

NOTES

1. Joseph Campbell, *The Hero with a Thousand Faces* (Princeton: Princeton University Press, Bollingen Series XVII, 1949; 2d ed., 1968).

2. Howard A. Berry and Linda A. Chisholm, *Service-Learning in Higher Education Around the World: An Initial Look* (New York: The International Partnership for Service-Learning, 1999), 9–23.

3. Campbell, 30.

4. Donald Keene, *Travelers of a Hundred Ages* (New York: Henry Holt and Company, Inc., 1989), 4.

5. Ibid., 2.

6. Joan Didion, *Slouching Towards Bethlehem* (New York: Farrar, Straus & Giroux, 1968), 135.

7. Campbell, 51.

8. Ibid.

9. Ibid., 77.

10. A. L. Basham, trans., *The Wonder That Was India* (New York: Macmillan, 1954). Quoted in Octavio Paz, *In Light of India* (New York: Harcourt Brace & Company, 1995), 139.

11. Campbell, 193.

12. Ibid.

13. Percy Bysshe Shelley, *Prometheus Unbound,* lines 573–574, written in 1819, published in the first edition of the Collected Works, 1839, quoted from *John Keats and Percy Bysshe Shelley: Complete Poetical Works with the Explanatory Notes of Shelley's Poems by Mrs. Shelley* (New York: Carlton House, n.d.), 293.

Annotated Bibliography

Jane Addams

Addams, Jane. *Twenty Years at Hull-House*. 1910. Reprint, New
    York: Penguin Putnam, 1998.

Jane Addams was born on September 6, 1860, in Cedarville,
Illinois. After attending Rockford College and receiving her B.A.
degree in 1882, she entered the Woman's Medical College of
Philadelphia. Because of illness she had to leave medical school,
and subsequently made several trips to Europe. On one such
trip, in 1888, she learned about the social experiment of
"settlement" on a visit to Toynbee Hall in London. She and
two colleagues opened Hull-House in Chicago in 1889 and there
developed the model of collective living and social action that
came to be known as the settlement house. She became a
crusader for social Justice — particularly for decent living and
working conditions — in Chicago and nationally as well. Jane
Addams and her wide network of friends and colleagues had
a profound influence on social reform and legislation in the
United States during the early decades of the twentieth century.
An advocate for peace, Addams was a founder in 1915 and
first president of the Women's International League for Peace
and Freedom. In recognition of her work for peace throughout
the world, she was awarded the Nobel Peace Prize in 1931. In
addition to *Twenty Years at Hull-House*, she was the author of
several other books, including *Democracy and Social Ethics* (1902),
The Spirit of Youth and City Streets (1930), and *My Friend, Julia
Lathrop* (1935). Jane Addams died in Chicago on May 21, 1935.

Frontispiece

EMILY BRONSON CONGER

Conger, Emily Bronson. *An Ohio Woman in the Philippines.*
Akron, Ohio: Press of Richard Leighton, 1904.

Sometime around 1897, well-to-do San Franciscan Emily
Bronson Conger, then a widow with three grown sons, accepted
an appointment from the Secretary of War to go as a nurse to
the Philippines. But, as she herself freely admits, "I preferred
to be under no obligation to render service." Her motivation
was to be near her son who was serving as a lieutenant in the
occupying American army.

Although she complained, "My health was poor and my
strength uncertain," in fact in the three to five years she spent
in Asia she proved herself remarkably strong of body, mind,
and spirit. She traveled not only in the Philippines but in China,
Japan, and Hawaii, and at each port of call she was observant
and curious, producing an engaging diary of her experiences.

Despite her reluctance to serve, Emily Bronson Conger became
a giver as well, using her skills of osteopathy for the benefit of
American soldiers and Filipinos alike.

She lived on the edge of danger, as there were frequent sallies
by Philippine "insurrectos" against U.S. military and civilian
colonialsts. In addition, there were earthquakes, monsoons, a
shipwreck, illness, heat, and mosquitoes for her to battle.

Despite occasional protestations in her journal, the overwhelming sense is that she loved her adventure. Originally from
Ohio, she possessed the limitations and virtues common to her
upbringing and held firmly to the values of the heartland, the
civic religion of Protestant Christianity, intense patriotism, and
devotion to family. Happily for her, these beliefs did not hinder
her appreciation of the life, peoples, and cultures of Asia.

PAUL COWAN

Cowan, Paul. *The Making of an Un-American: A Dialogue with Experience.* New York: Viking Press, 1970.

When Paul Cowan, schooled at Choate ('58) and Harvard, joined the Peace Corps in 1966, the United States was in the throes of the Civil Rights movement and the Vietnam War protests were gathering steam daily. People on all sides of all the questions were angry and blaming the government for all that ailed them and society. Paul Cowan was no exception, only that he was more articulate than most.

Chosen to go with his wife Rachel to Ecuador to serve the cause of justice with the newly formed United States Peace Corps, Cowan found little to praise and a lot to criticize, returning home to write a blistering account of his experience.

Times have changed since Cowan signed off on his book, *The Making of an Un-American.* The Peace Corps, only four years old at the time of his joining, has learned and adjusted its selection and processes. Peace Corps volunteers are now instructed differently on ways of working with the community, and the nations receiving volunteers have changed as well.

Paul Cowan's story is revealing of the intersection between personal life history and the historical moment. He both was shaped by and helped to shape his times.

SANA HASAN

Hasan, Sana. *Enemy in the Promised Land: An Egyptian Woman's Journey into Israel.* New York: Pantheon Books, 1986.

Sana Hasan grew up in Alexandria, Egypt, the daughter of a wealthy and prominent Arab family. Her father was a distinguished diplomat who, among other positions, served as Ambassador to the United States.

In 1973, Hasan arrived in the United States to register for her first courses at Harvard leading to a Ph.D. in political science.

> A few weeks later there was war between Egypt and Israel. With every day of war, the classroom theorizing on international relations seemed more irrelevant, as did the nightly television news broadcasts, which offered the spectacle of Arabs and Israelis killing each other for the entertainment of civilized Western viewers...Shortly thereafter, I went to the Israeli consulate to apply for a visa.
>
> *Enemy in the Promised Land*, 13

Thus began her life's work of trying to understand and interpret the nation of Israel, which she had been taught to despise and fear.

In 1984 she was awarded her Ph.D. by Harvard. She co-authored with Amos Elon *Between Enemies*, and has written on the Middle East for the *New York Times* and the *New York Review of Books*. At the time of the publication of the book excerpted here, Dr. Hasan was a visiting scholar at Hebrew University's Institute for Advanced Studies in Jerusalem.

LANGSTON HUGHES

Hughes, Langston. *The Big Sea.* 1940. Reprint, New York: Thunder's Mouth Press, 1986.

Langston Hughes (1902–1967), poet, novelist, essayist, short story writer, and playwright, was called by Carl Van Vechten "the US Negro poet laureate." Hughes shares the stage only with Claude McKay as the preeminent writer of the Harlem Renaissance. Hughes's two-volume autobiography, *The Big Sea* and *I Wonder as I Wander* (1956) is a remarkable piece of social history.

Hughes's father, estranged from Hughes's mother, moved to Mexico to escape segregationist policies in the U.S., and in Mexico successfully passed the bar examination and practiced law. He disappeared from young Langston's life, then re-appeared, urging his son to join him in Mexico. Langston came to love Mexico, but his living there was never easy as long as he was with his father.

Langston finally convinced his father to support his study at Columbia University. But as his journal records, his year of college was fraught with frustrations, and at the year's end he set sail for Africa. Through his journeys—to Mexico, New York, and Africa—his writing took shape, his first poems were published, and he began to receive the public recognition his talent so richly deserved.

JAMES BOSWELL AND SAMUEL JOHNSON

Boswell, James. *A Journal of a Tour to the Hebrides with Samuel Johnson, LL.D*. 1785. Reprint, London: J. M. Dent and Sons, 1928.

Johnson, Samuel. *A Journey to the Western Islands of Scotland*. 1775. Reprint, London: Chapman and Dodd, 1924.

Rogers, Pat, ed. *Johnson and Boswell in Scotland*. New Haven and London: Yale University Press, 1993.

Poet Anna Seward wrote of Samuel Johnson's and James Boswell's journals of their trip through Scotland, "In one [Johnson's] we perceive, through the medium of solemn and sublime eloquence, in what light Scotland, her nobles, her professors, and her chieftains appeared to the august wanderer: in the other [Boswell's] how the growling philosopher appeared to them." (Quoted in Rogers, x)

The names of Samuel Johnson (1709–1784) and James Boswell (1740–1795) are forever linked. Johnson, compiler of the English dictionary (published in 1755) which brought him un-precedented fame, was a man of letters, an essayist, poet, biographer, and moralist in the literary world of eighteenth century England. Boswell, thirty-one years his junior, became Johnson's friend, traveling companion, and biographer extraordinaire.

In 1773, they undertook a journey to Scotland, the land of Boswell's birth. The titles of their respective books—Johnson's *A Journey to the Western Islands of Scotland* and Boswell's *The Journal of a Tour to the Hebrides with Samuel Johnson*—tell all. For Johnson, the focus was Scotland; for Boswell, the focus was Johnson.

Their trip was, in some ways, a reversal of the Grand Tour which the English, wishing to be pronounced "educated," made of the Contintent. Boswell had made such a trip himself, claiming that as a result he was "a citizen of the world." For Johnson, the trip to Scotland was his first out of England, having been too poor as a young man to partake in the rite of passage of the privileged classes.

Scotland at the time of their journey had not yet been romanticized and publicized by the novels of Sir Walter Scott. For Johnson and Boswell, it was a trip to a harsh and as yet unfrequented environment, one that they relished, one from which they learned, and about which they wrote, leaving us with accounts that are literary masterpieces. (See Rogers, i–x.)

Johnson and Boswell are here presented together because they demonstrate dramatically how differently two people may view the same experience. The journey, even among trusted intimates, is always the hero's own.

MARY KINGSLEY

Kingsley, Mary. *Travels in West Africa.* 1897. Reprint, London: Virago Press, 1982.

Travels in West Africa is Mary Kingsley's record of her two journeys, made in 1893 at age thirty and again in 1894. Her keen observations and her wit have made her book a classic in the fields of travel literature and African culture.

As Elizabeth Claridge notes in the introduction to the fifth edition of the book, "Few women have stepped so abruptly from conventional circumstances into the unknown."

Kingsley, the daughter of a physician and naturalist and niece of novelist Charles Kingsley, had never been abroad before boarding the ship which would take her to the land then known to Englishmen as "the dark continent." Her interests included fish and insects — she had studied the work of Charles Darwin — and tribal customs and fetish.

Upon return to England and with the publication of her book, she became widely sought for lecturing and for writing articles. In March of 1900 she went to South Africa to nurse Boer prisoners of war and there caught enteric fever and died. The Mary Kingsley Society of West Africa, later called the African Society, was established in her memory.

KATHLEEN NORRIS

Norris, Kathleen. *Dakota: A Spiritual Geography.* New York: Houghton Mifflin Company, 1993.

Kathleen Norris, a struggling New York City writer, inherited a house in Lemmon, South Dakota (population: 1,600), where her mother had grown up and where she herself had spent many childhood summers. With her poet husband, she moved into the house, expecting to be there but a few years to clear up the farm interests. Instead, they stayed, growing to love the prairie, life in the small town, and the quiet, reflective time which nourished them as writers.

Through the choice of this place, so contrary to twentieth-century ambitions and trends, Norris embarked on her own spiritual journey, challenged and enriched by the vast space and harsh weather of the Great Plains, by the people of the small towns and farms; by the life and worship of the Benedictine monks who established their monastery in South Dakota; and through her reflections on her life and theirs.

She is author of two books of poetry: *Falling Off* (1971) and *The Middle of the World* (1981); as well as *The Cloister Walk* (1997) and *Amazing Grace: A Vocabulary of Faith* (1999).

OCTAVIO PAZ

Paz, Octavio. *In Light of India*. Translated by Eliot Weinberger. New York: Harcourt Brace and Company, 1995.

The Mexican poet, philosopher, and essayist Octavio Paz (1914–1998) was awarded the Nobel Prize for Literature in 1990. His works include: *The Labyrinth of Solitude, The Other Mexico, Alternating Current, The Bow and the Lyre, Children of the Mire, Conjunctions and Disjunctions, Selected Poems, One Earth, Four or Five Worlds, Collected Poems 1957–1987, Convergences, Sunstone, The Other Voice, In Search of the Present, Essays on Mexican Art,* and *The Double Flame.*

In 1951, Paz first traveled to India as an attaché in the Mexican Embassy. In 1962, he returned as Mexico's Ambassador to India, a position he held for six years.

In Light of India is Octavio Paz's reflection on the religions, art, and history of India. It contains fascinating comparisons between Mexico and India, and describes specifics of the cultures in the broadest possible perspectives. His book is an extraordinary example of a search for the roots of a culture, and an examination of the persistence of cultural characteristics that shape peoples and nations.

Anthony Winkler

Winkler, Anthony C. *Going Home to Teach*. Kingston, Jamaica: Kingston Publishers, 1995.

A white Jamaican, Anthony Winkler emigrated to the United States — to Los Angeles — as a young man to seek fame and fortune. For thirteen years he remained in the United States, and was a successful university teacher and author, with three college textbooks to his credit.

But in 1975, just when middle-class Jamaicans were fleeing the socialist government of Michael Manley, Winkler, with his American wife, Cathy, chose to go home to teach at a rural teacher training college in the hills of Jamaica.

He is the author of *The Painted Canoe* and *The Lunatic*, both of which are also now motion pictures, and *The Great Yacht Race*. His current home is in Atlanta, where he lives with his wife and family.

Winkler writes, "I am keenly interested in the cultural chasm that exists between people of different countries, and I have mainly aimed my writing at that theme. Odd things always seem to be popping about me in the United States, and I must periodically run home to Jamaica for a taste of normalcy." (Quotation on the book jacket of *Going Home to Teach*.)